THE BOOK OF
AMERICAN NEGRO POETRY

James Weldon Johnson

THE AUTOBIOGRAPHY OF AN EX-COLORED MAN

FIFTY YEARS AND OTHER POEMS

THE BOOK OF AMERICAN NEGRO SPIRITUALS
(Edited with a Preface)

THE SECOND BOOK OF AMERICAN NEGRO SPIRITUALS
(Edited with a Preface)

GOD'S TROMBONES—SEVEN NEGRO SERMONS IN VERSE

BLACK MANHATTAN

SAINT PETER RELATES AN INCIDENT OF THE
RESURRECTION DAY

NEGRO AMERICANS, WHAT NOW?

ALONG THIS WAY

SELECTED POEMS

THE BOOK OF
AMERICAN NEGRO
POETRY

Edited by

JAMES WELDON JOHNSON

REVISED EDITION

HBJ

A Harvest/HBJ Book
Harcourt Brace Jovanovich, Publishers
San Diego   New York   London

Copyright 1931, 1922 by Harcourt Brace Jovanovich, Inc.
Copyright renewed 1959 by Mrs. Grace Nail Johnson
Copyright renewed 1950 by Grace Johnson

Library of Congress Cataloging in Publication Data
Main entry under title:
The Book of American Negro poetry.
   (A Harvest/HBJ book)
   Reprint. Originally published: Harcourt Brace & World, 1969, c1959.
   Bibliography: p.
   Includes index.
   1. American poetry—Afro-American authors.   I. Johnson, James Weldon, 1871-1938.
PS591.N4B62 1983   811'.008'0896073   83-8442
ISBN 0-15-613539-6

Printed in the United States of America
DEFGHIJ

CONTENTS

THE BOOK OF
AMERICAN NEGRO POETRY

PREFACE TO THE REVISED EDITION

WHEN this book was compiled, only ten years ago, the conception of the Negro as a creator of art was so new, indeed so unformed, that I felt it was necessary to make a rather extended introduction in presenting to the public an anthology of poetry by Negro writers. And so, forty-eight pages were devoted to calling attention to the main contributions which the Negro had already made to our common cultural store, and to setting forth a modest claim for his powers of artistic creation and expression.

Within this brief period the introduction to the original edition of the book has become primarily a matter of historical data. Its statements, claims, and forecasts are today, for the most part, accepted facts. Within the past decade there has grown a general recognition that the Negro is a contributor to American life not only of material but of artistic, cultural, and spiritual values; that in the making and shaping of American civilization he is an active force, a giver as well as a receiver, a creator as well as a creature.

The statement made in the original preface regarding the limitations of Negro dialect as a poetic medium [1] has, it may be said, come to be regarded as more or less canonical. It is as sound today as when it was written ten years ago; and its implications are more apparent. It calls for no modifications, but it can well be amplified here. The passing of traditional dialect as a medium for Negro poets is complete. The passing of traditional dialect as poetry is almost com-

[1] See pages 41, 42.

3

plete. Today even the reader is conscious that almost all poetry in the conventionalized dialect is either based upon the minstrel traditions of Negro life, traditions that had but slight relation—often no relation at all—to actual Negro life, or is permeated with artificial sentiment. It is now realized both by the poets and by their public that as an instrument for poetry the dialect has only two main stops, humor and pathos.

That this is not a shortcoming inherent in the dialect as dialect is demonstrated by the wide compass it displays in its use in the folk creations. The limitation is due to conventions that have been fixed upon the dialect and the conformity to them by individual writers. Negro dialect poetry had its origin in the minstrel traditions, and a persisting pattern was set. When the individual writer attempted to get away from that pattern, the fixed conventions allowed him only to slip over into a slough of sentimentality. These conventions were not broken for the simple reason that the individual writers wrote chiefly to entertain an outside audience, and in concord with its stereotyped ideas about the Negro. And herein lies the vital distinction between them and the folk creators, who wrote solely to please and express themselves.

Several of the poets of the younger group, notably Langston Hughes and Sterling A. Brown, *do* use a dialect; but it is not the dialect of the comic minstrel tradition or of the sentimental plantation tradition; it is the common, racy, living, authentic speech of the Negro in certain phases of real life.

It is not out of place to say that it is more than regrettable that the traditional dialect was forced into the narrow and unnatural literary mold it occupies. If Negro poets, writing sincerely to express their race and for their race, had been the first to develop and fix it, they might have been able to make of it something comparable to the literary medium that Burns made of the Scottish dialect. If he addressed himself to the task, the Aframerican poet might in time break the old conventional mold; but I don't think he will do it, because I don't think he considers it now worth the effort.

The original preface also gives a summarized account of the miscellaneous group of Negro poets from Phillis Wheatley, who published a volume of poems in 1773, down to Paul Laurence Dunbar (1872-1906). The selections in the main section of the first edition of the book represented two periods: the first embracing the poets of the Dunbar school and other writers down to the outbreak of the World War; the second embracing the group that emerged during the war. Since the original publication of the book a third group has arisen. The preëminent figures in this younger group are Countee Cullen, who published his first volume, *Color*, in 1925, and Langston Hughes, who published his first volume, *The Weary Blues*, in 1926.

The rise of the World War group involved a revolt against the traditions of Negro dialect poetry, against stereotyped humorous-pathetic patterns, against sentimental and supplicatory moods; it involved an attempt to express the feelings of disillusionment and bitterness the American Negro was then experiencing, and out of it there came poetry of protest, rebellion, and despair. The rise of the younger group involved a revolt against "propaganda," an effort to get away from "race problem" poetry, an attempt to break through racial barriers that hedge in even art in the United States, a desire to be simply poets.

The poets of the younger group have not succeeded fundamentally in what they undertook to do; in the main they, too, are writing race-conscious poetry, poetry that is, perhaps, more highly charged with race than that of the World War group. But the best of them have found an approach to "race" that is different. Their approach is less direct, less obvious than that of their predecessors, and thereby they have secured a gain in subtlety of power and, probably, in ultimate effectiveness. Some of the younger poets made a futile effort to ignore "race" and all it implies in the United States, to deny intellectually its existence, with the result that they either produced race-conscious poetry of the worst sort—poetry of bombast and braggadocio—or failed to produce anything vital. It is interesting to note how Countee Cullen, Langston Hughes, Sterling A. Brown, Helene Johnson, Arna Bontemps, Frank Horne, Waring Cuney, Gwendolyn Bennett, and others of the group react to this matter of "race." While they have not written exclusively poetry rising out of race-consciousness, it is manifest that their best efforts spring from that source.

Several of the group have dug down into the genuine folk stuff—I mention genuine folk stuff in contradistinction to the artificial folk stuff of the dialect school—to get their material; for example, Langston Hughes has gone to such folk sources as the blues and the work songs; Sterling A. Brown has gone to Negro folk epics and ballads like "Stagolee," "John Henry," "Casey Jones," and "Long Gone John." These are unfailing sources of material for authentic poetry. I myself did a similar thing in writing *God's Trombones*. I went back to the genuine folk stuff that clings around the old-time Negro preacher, material which had many times been worked into something both artificial and false.

I have no intention of depreciating the poetry not stimu-
lated by a sense of race that Aframerican poets have written;
much of it is as high as the average standard of American
poetry and some of it higher; but not in all of it do I find a
single poem possessing the power and artistic finality found
in the best of the poems rising out of racial conflict and con-
tact. All of which is merely a confirmation of the axiom
that an artist accomplishes his best when working at his
best with the material he knows best. And up to this time,
at least, "race" is perforce the thing the American Negro
poet knows best. Assuredly, the time will come when he will
know other things as well as he now knows "race," and will,
perhaps, feel them as deeply; or, to state this in another way,
the time should come when he will not have to know "race"
so well and feel it so deeply. But even now he can escape the
sense of being hampered if, standing on his racial founda-
tion, he strives to fashion something that rises above mere
race and reaches out to the universal in truth and beauty.

The writers of the younger group are developing. The
greater part of their work still lies within the compass of the
old circle, but they possess a greater self-sufficiency than any
generation before them and are freer from sensitiveness to
the approbation or deprecation of their white environment.
It is for the purpose of including the writers of this group
that this enlarged edition of *The Book of American Negro
Poetry* is published. (In this book the term, "American
Negro poetry," is used solely because it is more concise—
even if less expository—than the expression, "poetry written
by American Negroes.")

The book now contains selections from the work of forty
writers, with a summary in the original preface of the work
of the more important ones prior to Paul Laurence Dunbar.

The sketches of the poets included have been made critical as well as biographical, and a list of references for supplementary reading has been added.

The work of revision has been done during the fellowship granted me by the Julius Rosenwald Fund.

I wish to record grateful acknowledgment to:

Harper and Brothers, for permission to reprint the poems selected from *Color*, *Copper Sun*, and *The Black Christ*, by Countee Cullen.

Alfred A. Knopf, Inc., for permission to reprint the poems selected from *The Weary Blues* and *Fine Clothes to the Jew*, by Langston Hughes.

The Viking Press for permission to reprint selections from *God's Trombones*, by James Weldon Johnson.

The Crisis, *Opportunity*, *The Saturday Evening Quill*, and *Folk-Say*, for uncollected poems published in their pages.

To Miss Richetta G. Randolph I wish to express appreciation for her valuable assistance in the preparation of the manuscript for the press.

JAMES WELDON JOHNSON

New York City
1931

PREFACE TO THE FIRST EDITION

THERE is, perhaps, a better excuse for giving an Anthology of American Negro Poetry to the public than can be offered for many of the anthologies that have recently been issued. The public, generally speaking, does not know that there are American Negro poets—to supply this lack of information is, alone, a work worthy of somebody's effort.

Moreover, the matter of Negro poets and the production of literature by the colored people in this country involves more than supplying information that is lacking. It is a matter which has a direct bearing on the most vital of American problems.

A people may become great through many means, but there is only one measure by which its greatness is recognized and acknowledged. The final measure of the greatness of all peoples is the amount and standard of the literature and art they have produced. The world does not know that a people is great until that people produces great literature and art. No people that has produced great literature and art has ever been looked upon by the world as distinctly inferior.

The status of the Negro in the United States is more a question of national mental attitude toward the race than of actual conditions. And nothing will do more to change that mental attitude and raise his status than a demonstration of intellectual parity by the Negro through the production of literature and art.

Is there likelihood that the American Negro will be able to do this? There is, for the good reason that he possesses the innate powers. He has the emotional endowment, the originality and artistic conception, and, what is more important, the power of creating that which has universal appeal and influence.

I make here what may appear to be a more startling statement by saying that the Negro has already proved the possession of these powers by being the creator of the only things artistic that have yet sprung from American soil and been universally acknowledged as distinctive American products.[1]

These creations by the American Negro may be summed up under four heads. The first two are the Uncle Remus stories, which were collected by Joel Chandler Harris, and the "spirituals" or slave songs, to which the Fisk Jubilee Singers made the public and the musicians of both the United States and Europe listen. The Uncle Remus stories constitute the greatest body of folk lore that America has produced, and the "spirituals" the greatest body of folk song. I shall speak of the "spirituals" later because they are more than folk songs, for in them the Negro sounded the depths, if he did not scale the heights, of music.

The other two creations are the cakewalk and ragtime. We do not need to go very far back to remember when cakewalking was the rage in the United States, Europe and South America. Society in this country and royalty abroad spent time in practicing the intricate steps. Paris pronounced it the "poetry of motion." The popularity of the cakewalk passed away but its influence remained. The influence can be seen today on any American stage where there is dancing.

The influence which the Negro has exercised on the art of dancing in this country has been almost absolute. For

[1] This statement should probably be modified by the inclusion of American skyscraper architecture. (*Editor, 1931.*)

generations the "buck and wing" and the "stop-time"
dances, which are strictly Negro, have been familiar to
American theater audiences. A few years ago the public
discovered the "turkey trot," the "eagle rock," "ballin' the
jack," and several other varieties that started the modern
dance craze. These dances were quickly followed by the
"tango," a dance originated by the Negroes of Cuba and
later transplanted to South America. (This fact is attested
by no less authority than Vicente Blasco Ibañez in his *Four
Horsemen of the Apocalypse*.) Half the floor space in the
country was then turned over to dancing, and highly paid
exponents sprang up everywhere. The most noted, Mr. Ver-
non Castle, and, by the way, an Englishman, never danced
except to the music of a colored band, and he never failed
to state to his audiences that most of his dances had long
been done by "your colored people," as he put it.

Any one who witnesses a musical production in which
there is dancing cannot fail to notice the Negro stamp on all
the movements; a stamp which even the great vogue of Rus-
sian dances that swept the country about the time of the
popular dance craze could not affect. That peculiar sway-
ing of the shoulders which you see done everywhere by the
blond girls of the chorus is nothing more than a movement
from the Negro dance referred to above, the "eagle rock."
Occasionally the movement takes on a suggestion of the now
outlawed "shimmy."

As for Ragtime, I go straight to the statement that it is
the one artistic production by which America is known the
world over. It has been all-conquering. Everywhere it is
hailed as "American music."

For a dozen years or so there has been a steady tendency
to divorce Ragtime from the Negro; in fact, to take from

him the credit of having originated it. Probably the younger
people of the present generation do not know that Ragtime
is of Negro origin. The change wrought in Ragtime and
the way in which it is accepted by the country have been
brought about chiefly through the change which has grad-
ually been made in the words and stories accompanying the
music. Once the text of all Ragtime songs was written in
Negro dialect, and was about Negroes in the cabin or in the
cotton field or on the levee or at a jubilee or on Sixth Avenue
or at a ball, and about their love affairs. Today, only a small
proportion of Ragtime songs relate at all to the Negro. The
truth is, Ragtime is now national rather than racial. But that
does not abolish in any way the claim of the American Negro
as its originator.

Ragtime music was originated by colored piano players
in the questionable resorts of St. Louis, Memphis, and other
Mississippi River towns. These men did not know any more
about the theory of music than they did about the theory of
the universe. They were guided by their natural musical
instinct and talent, but above all by the Negro's extraor-
dinary sense of rhythm. Any one who is familiar with Rag-
time may note that its chief charm is not in melody, but in
rhythms. These players often improvised crude and, at times,
vulgar words to fit the music. This was the beginning of
the Ragtime song.

Ragtime music got its first popular hearing at Chicago
during the World's Fair in that city. From Chicago it
made its way to New York, and then started on its universal
triumph.

The earliest Ragtime songs, like Topsy, "jes' grew."
Some of these earliest songs were taken down by white men,
the words slightly altered or changed, and published under

the names of the arrangers. They sprang into immediate popularity and earned small fortunes. The first to become widely known was "The Bully," a levee song which had been long used by roustabouts along the Mississippi. It was introduced in New York by Miss May Irwin, and gained instant popularity. Another one of these "jes' grew" songs was one which for a while disputed for place with Yankee Doodle; perhaps, disputes it even today. That song was "A Hot Time in the Old Town Tonight"; introduced and made popular by the colored regimental bands during the Spanish-American War.

Later there came along a number of colored men who were able to transcribe the old songs and write original ones. I was, about that time, writing words to music for the music show stage in New York. I was collaborating with my brother, J. Rosamond Johnson, and the late Bob Cole. I remember that we appropriated about the last one of the old "jes' grew" songs. It was a song which had been sung for years all through the South. The words were unprintable, but the tune was irresistible, and belonged to nobody. We took it, re-wrote the verses, telling an entirely different story from the original, left the chorus as it was, and published the song, at first under the name of "Will Handy." It became very popular with college boys, especially at football games, and perhaps still is. The song was "Oh, Didn't He Ramble!"

In the beginning, and for quite a while, almost all of the Ragtime songs that were deliberately composed were the work of colored writers. Now, the colored composers, even in this particular field, are greatly outnumbered by the white.

The reader might be curious to know if the "jes' grew" songs have ceased to grow. No, they have not; they are

growing all the time. The country has lately been flooded
with several varieties of "The Blues." These "Blues," too,
had their origin in Memphis, and the towns along the Mis-
sissippi. They are a sort of lament of a lover who is feeling
"blue" over the loss of his sweetheart. The "Blues" of Mem-
phis have been adulterated so much on Broadway that they
have lost their pristine hue. But whenever you hear a piece
of music which has a strain like this in it:

you will know you are listening to something which be-
longed originally to Beale Avenue, Memphis, Tennessee.
The original "Memphis Blues," so far as it can be credited
to a composer, must be credited to Mr. W. C. Handy, a col-
ored musician of Memphis.

As illustrations of the genuine Ragtime song in the mak-
ing, I quote the words of two that were popular with the
Southern colored soldiers in France. Here is the first:

Mah mammy's lyin' in her grave,
   Mah daddy done run away,
Mah sister's married a gamblin' man,
   An' I've done gone astray.
Yes, I've done gone astray, po' boy,
   An' I've done gone astray,
Mah sister's married a gamblin' man,
   An' I've done gone astray, po' boy.

These lines are crude, but they contain something of real
poetry, of that elusive thing which nobody can define and
that you can only tell is there when you feel it. You
cannot read these lines without becoming reflective and
feeling sorry for "Po' Boy."

Now, take in this word picture of utter dejection:

> I'm jes' as misabul as I can be,
> I'm unhappy even if I am free,
> I'm feelin' down, I'm feelin' blue;
> I wander 'round, don't know what to do.
> I'm go'n lay mah haid on de railroad line;
> Let de B. & O. come and pacify mah min'.

These lines are, no doubt, one of the many versions of
the famous "Blues." They are also crude, but they go
straight to the mark. The last two lines move with the
swiftness of all great tragedy.

In spite of the bans which musicians and music teachers
have placed on it, the people still demand and enjoy Rag-
time. In fact, there is not a corner of the civilized world in
which it is not known and liked. And this proves its origi-
nality, for if it were an imitation, the people of Europe, at
least, would not have found it a novelty. And it is proof
of a more important thing, it is proof that Ragtime possesses
the vital spark, the power to appeal universally, without
which any artistic production, no matter how approved its
form may be, is dead.

Of course, there are those who will deny that Ragtime
is an artistic production. American musicians, especially, in-
stead of investigating Ragtime, dismiss it with a contemptu-
ous word. But this has been the course of scholasticism in
every branch of art. Whatever new thing the people like is

pooh-poohed; whatever is popular is regarded as not worth while. The fact is, nothing great or enduring in music has ever sprung full-fledged from the brain of any master; the best he gives the world he gathers from the hearts of the people, and runs it through the alembic of his genius.

Ragtime deserves serious attention. There is a lot of colorless and vicious imitation, but there is enough that is genuine. In one composition alone, "The Memphis Blues," the musician will find not only great melodic beauty, but a polyphonic structure that is amazing.

It is obvious that Ragtime has influenced and, in a large measure, become our popular music; but not many would know that it has influenced even our religious music. Those who are familiar with gospel hymns can at once see this influence if they will compare the songs of thirty years ago, such as "In the Sweet Bye and Bye," "The Ninety and Nine," etc., with the up-to-date, syncopated tunes that are sung in Sunday Schools, Christian Endeavor Societies, Y.M.C.A.'s and like gatherings today.

Ragtime has not only influenced American music, it has influenced American life; indeed, it has saturated American life. It has become the popular medium for our national expression musically. And who can say that it does not express the blare and jangle and the surge, too, of our national spirit?

Any one who doubts that there is a peculiar heel-tickling, smile-provoking, joy-awakening, response-compelling charm in Ragtime needs only to hear a skillful performer play the genuine article, needs only to listen to its bizarre harmonies, its audacious resolutions often consisting of an abrupt jump from one key to another, its intricate rhythms in which the accents fall in the most unexpected places but in which the

fundamental beat is never lost, in order to be convinced. I
believe it has its place as well as the music which draws from
us sighs and tears.

Now, these dances which I have referred to and Rag-
time music may be lower forms of art, but they are evidence
of a power that will some day be applied to the higher forms.
And even now we need not stop at the Negro's accomplish-
ment through these lower forms. In the "spirituals," or slave
songs, the Negro has given America not only its only folk
songs, but a mass of noble music. I never think of this music
but that I am struck by the wonder, the miracle of its pro-
duction. How did the men who originated these songs man-
age to do it? The sentiments are easily accounted for; they
are, for the most part, taken from the Bible. But the melo-
dies, where did they come from? Some of them so weirdly
sweet, and others so wonderfully strong. Take, for instance,
"Go Down, Moses"; I doubt that there is a stronger theme
in the whole musical literature of the world.

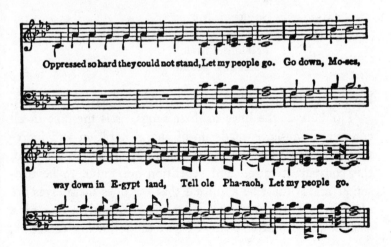

Oppressed so hard they could not stand, Let my people go. Go down, Mo-ses,

way down in E-gypt land,   Tell ole Pha-raoh, Let my people go.

It is to be noted that whereas the chief characteristic of Ragtime is rhythm, the chief characteristic of the "spirituals" is melody. The melodies of "Steal Away to Jesus," "Swing Low Sweet Chariot," "Nobody Knows de Trouble I See," "I Couldn't Hear Nobody Pray," "Deep River," "O, Freedom Over Me," and many others of these songs possess a beauty that is—what shall I say? poignant. In the riotous rhythms of Ragtime the Negro expressed his irrepressible buoyancy, his keen response to the sheer joy of living; in the "spirituals" he voiced his sense of beauty and his deep religious feeling.

Naturally, not as much can be said for the words of these songs as for the music. Most of the songs are religious. Some of them are songs expressing faith and endurance and a longing for freedom. In the religious songs, the sentiments and often the entire lines are taken bodily from the Bible. However, there is no doubt that some of these religious songs have a meaning apart from the Biblical text. It is evident that the opening lines of "Go Down, Moses,"

> Go down, Moses,
> 'Way down in Egypt land;
> Tell old Pharaoh,
> Let my people go.

have a significance beyond the bondage of Israel in Egypt.

The bulk of the lines to these songs, as is the case in all communal music, is made up of choral iteration and incremental repetition of the leader's lines. If the words are read, this constant iteration and repetition are found to be tiresome; and it must be admitted that the lines themselves are often very trite. And, yet, there is frequently revealed a flash of real primitive poetry. I give the following examples:

Sometimes I feel like an eagle in de air.

You may bury me in de East,
You may bury me in de West,
But I'll hear de trumpet sound
In-a dat mornin'.

I know de moonlight, I know de starlight;
I lay dis body down.
I walk in de moonlight, I walk in de starlight;
I lay dis body down.
I know de graveyard, I know de graveyard,
When I lay dis body down.
I walk in de graveyard, I walk troo de graveyard
To lay dis body down.

I lay in de grave an' stretch out my arms;
I lay dis body down.
I go to de judgment in de evenin' of de day
When I lay dis body down.
An' my soul an' yo soul will meet in de day
When I lay dis body down.

Regarding the line, "I lay in de grave an' stretch out my arms," Col. Thomas Wentworth Higginson of Boston, one of the first to give these slave songs serious study, said: "Never, it seems to me, since man first lived and suffered, was his infinite longing for peace uttered more plaintively than in that line."

These Negro folk songs constitute a vast mine of material that has been neglected almost absolutely. The only white writers who have in recent years given adequate attention and study to this music, that I know of, are Mr. H. E. Krehbiel and Mrs. Natalie Curtis Burlin. We have our native composers denying the worth and importance of this music, and trying to manufacture grand opera out of so-called Indian themes.

But there is a great hope for the development of this music, and that hope is the Negro himself. A worthy beginning has already been made by Burleigh, Cook, Johnson, and Dett. And there will yet come great Negro composers who will take this music and voice through it not only the soul of their race, but the soul of America.

And does it not seem odd that this greatest gift of the Negro has been the most neglected of all he possesses? Money and effort have been expended upon his development in every direction except this. This gift has been regarded as a kind of side show, something for occasional exhibition; wherein it is the touchstone, it is the magic thing, it is that by which the Negro can bridge all chasms. No persons, however hostile, can listen to Negroes singing this wonderful music without having their hostility melted down.

This power of the Negro to suck up the national spirit from the soil and create something artistic and original, which, at the same time, possesses the note of universal appeal, is due to a remarkable racial gift of adaptability; it is more than adaptability, it is a transfusive quality. And the Negro has exercised this transfusive quality not only here in America, where the race lives in large numbers, but in European countries, where the number has been almost infinitesimal.

Is it not curious to know that the greatest poet of Russia is Alexander Pushkin, a man of African descent; that the greatest romancer of France is Alexandre Dumas, a man of African descent; and that one of the greatest musicians of England is Coleridge-Taylor, a man of African descent?

The fact is fairly well known that the father of Dumas was a Negro of the French West Indies, and that the father of Coleridge-Taylor was a native-born African; but the facts concerning Pushkin's African ancestry are not so familiar.

When Peter the Great was Czar of Russia, some potentate presented him with a full-blooded Negro of gigantic size. Peter, the most eccentric ruler of modern times, dressed this Negro up in soldier clothes, christened him Hannibal, and made him a special body-guard.

But Hannibal had more than size, he had brain and ability. He not only looked picturesque and imposing in soldier clothes, he showed that he had in him the making of a real soldier. Peter recognized this, and eventually made him a general. He afterwards ennobled him, and Hannibal, later, married one of the ladies of the Russian court. This same Hannibal was great-grandfather of Pushkin, the national poet of Russia, the man who bears the same relation to Russian literature that Shakespeare bears to English literature.

I know the question naturally arises: If out of the few Negroes who have lived in France there came a Dumas; and out of the few Negroes who have lived in England there came a Coleridge-Taylor; and if from the man who was at the time, probably, the only Negro in Russia there sprang that country's national poet, why have not the millions of Negroes in the United States with all the emotional and artistic endowment claimed for them produced a Dumas, or a Coleridge-Taylor, or a Pushkin?

The question seems difficult, but there is an answer. The Negro in the United States is consuming all of his intellectual energy in this grueling race-struggle. And the same

statement may be made in a general way about the white
South. Why does not the white South produce literature
and art? The white South, too, is consuming all of its intel-
lectual energy in this lamentable conflict. Nearly all of the
mental efforts of the white South run through one narrow
channel. The life of every Southern white man and all of
his activities are impassably limited by the ever present
Negro problem. And that is why, as Mr. H. L. Mencken
puts it, in all that vast region, with its thirty or forty million
people and its territory as large as a half dozen Frances or
Germanys, there is not a single poet, not a serious historian,
not a creditable composer, not a critic good or bad, not a
dramatist dead or alive.[1]

But, even so, the American Negro has accomplished
something in pure literature. The list of those who have
done so would be surprising both by its length and the excel-
lence of the achievements. One of the great books written
in this country since the Civil War is the work of a colored
man, *The Souls of Black Folks*, by W. E. B. Du Bois.

Such a list begins with Phillis Wheatley. In 1761 a slave
ship landed a cargo of slaves in Boston. Among them was a
little girl seven or eight years of age. She attracted the
attention of John Wheatley, a wealthy gentleman of Boston,
who purchased her as a servant for his wife. Mrs. Wheatley
was a benevolent woman. She noticed the girl's quick mind
and determined to give her opportunity for its development.
Twelve years later Phillis published a volume of poems. The
book was brought out in London, where Phillis was for
several months an object of great curiosity and attention.

[1] This statement was quoted in 1921. The reader may consider for
himself the changes wrought in the decade. (*Editor, 1931.*)

Phillis Wheatley has never been given her rightful place in American literature. By some sort of conspiracy she is kept out of most of the books, especially the text-books on literature used in the schools. Of course, she is not a *great* American poet—and in her day there were no great American poets—but she is an important American poet. Her importance, if for no other reason, rests on the fact that, save one, she is the first in order of time of all the women poets of America. And she is among the first of all American poets to issue a volume.

It seems strange that the books generally give space to a mention of Urian Oakes, President of Harvard College, and to quotations from the crude and lengthy elegy which he published in 1667; and print examples from the execrable versified version of the Psalms made by the New England divines, and yet deny a place to Phillis Wheatley.

Here are the opening lines from the elegy by Oakes, which is quoted from in most of the books on American literature:

> Reader, I am no poet, but I grieve.
> Behold here what that passion can do,
> That forced a verse without Apollo's leave,
> And whether the learned sisters would or no.

There was no need for Urian to admit what his handiwork declared. But this from the versified Psalms is still worse, yet it is found in the books:

> The Lord's song sing can we? being
> in stranger's land, then let
> lose her skill my right hand if I
> Jerusalem forget.

Anne Bradstreet preceded Phillis Wheatley by a little over twenty years. She published her volume of poems, *The Tenth Muse*, in 1750. Let us strike a comparison between the two. Anne Bradstreet was a wealthy, cultivated Puritan girl, the daughter of Thomas Dudley, Governor of Bay Colony. Phillis, as we know, was a Negro slave girl born in Africa. Let us take them both at their best and in the same vein. The following stanza is from Anne's poem entitled "Contemplation":

> While musing thus with contemplation fed,
> And thousand fancies buzzing in my brain,
> The sweet tongued Philomel percht o'er my head,
> And chanted forth a most melodious strain,
> Which rapt me so with wonder and delight,
> I judged my hearing better than my sight,
> And wisht me wings with her awhile to take my flight.

And the following is from Phillis' poem entitled "Imagination":

> Imagination! who can sing thy force?
> Or who describe the swiftness of thy course?
> Soaring through air to find the bright abode,
> Th' empyreal palace of the thundering God,
> We on thy pinions can surpass the wind,
> And leave the rolling universe behind.
> From star to star the mental optics rove,
> Measure the skies, and range the realms above;
> There in one view we grasp the mighty whole,
> Or with new worlds amaze th' unbounded soul.

We do not think the black woman suffers much by comparison with the white. Thomas Jefferson said of Phillis:

"Religion has produced a Phillis Wheatley, but it could not produce a poet; her poems are beneath contempt." It is quite likely that Jefferson's criticism was directed more against religion than against Phillis' poetry. On the other hand, General George Washington wrote her with his own hand a letter in which he thanked her for a poem which she had dedicated to him. He later received her with marked courtesy at his camp at Cambridge.

It appears certain that Phillis was the first person to apply to George Washington the phrase, "First in peace." The phrase occurs in her poem addressed to "His Excellency, General George Washington," written in 1775. The encomium, "First in war, first in peace, first in the hearts of his countrymen," was originally used in the resolutions presented to Congress on the death of Washington, December, 1799.

Phillis Wheatley's poetry is the poetry of the Eighteenth Century. She wrote when Pope and Gray were supreme; it is easy to see that Pope was her model. Had she come under the influence of Wordsworth, Byron or Keats or Shelley, she would have done greater work. As it is, her work must not be judged by the work and standards of a later day, but by the work and standards of her own day and her own contemporaries. By this method of criticism she stands out as one of the important characters in the making of American literature, without any allowances for her sex or her antecedents.

According to *A Bibliographical Checklist of American Negro Poetry*, compiled by Mr. Arthur A. Schomburg, more than one hundred Negroes in the United States have published volumes of poetry ranging in size from pamphlets to books of from one hundred to three hundred pages. About

thirty of these writers fill in the gap between Phillis Wheat-
ley and Paul Laurence Dunbar. Just here it is of interest
to note that a Negro wrote and published a poem before
Phillis Wheatley arrived in this country from Africa. He
was Jupiter Hammon, a slave belonging to a Mr. Lloyd
of Queens-Village, Long Island. In 1760 Hammon pub-
lished a poem, eighty-eight lines in length, entitled "An
Evening Thought, Salvation by Christ, with Penettential
Cries." In 1788 he published "An Address to Miss Phillis
Wheatley, Ethiopian Poetess in Boston, who came from
Africa at eight years of age, and soon became acquainted
with the Gospel of Jesus Christ." These two poems do not
include all that Hammon wrote.

The poets between Phillis Wheatley and Dunbar must
be considered more in the light of what they attempted than
of what they accomplished. Many of them showed marked
talent, but barely a half dozen of them demonstrated even
mediocre mastery of technique in the use of poetic ma-
terial and forms. And yet there are several names that de-
serve mention. George M. Horton, Frances E. Harper,
James M. Bell and Alberry A. Whitman, all merit con-
sideration when due allowances are made for their limita-
tions in education, training and general culture. The limita-
tions of Horton were greater than those of either of the
others; he was born a slave in North Carolina in 1797, and
as a young man began to compose poetry without being able
to write it down. Later he received some instruction from
professors of the University of North Carolina, at which
institution he was employed as a janitor. He published a
volume of poems, *The Hope of Liberty*, in 1829.

Mrs. Harper, Bell, and Whitman would stand out if
only for the reason that each of them attempted sustained

work. Mrs. Harper published her first volume of poems in
1854, but later she published "Moses, a Story of the Nile,"
a poem which ran to 52 closely printed pages. Bell in 1864
published a poem of 28 pages in celebration of President
Lincoln's Emancipation Proclamation. In 1870 he pub-
lished a poem of 32 pages in celebration of the ratification
of the Fifteenth Amendment to the Constitution. Whitman
published his first volume of poems, a book of 253 pages, in
1877; but in 1884 he published "The Rape of Florida," an
epic poem written in four cantos and done in the Spen-
serian stanza, and which ran to 97 closely printed pages.
The poetry of both Mrs. Harper and of Whitman had a
large degree of popularity; one of Mrs. Harper's books went
through more than twenty editions.

Of these four poets, it is Whitman who reveals not only
the greatest imagination but also the more skillful workman-
ship. His lyric power at its best may be judged from the fol-
lowing stanza from the "Rape of Florida":

> "Come now, my love, the moon is on the lake;
> Upon the waters is my light canoe;
> Come with me, love, and gladsome oars shall make
> A music on the parting wave for you.
> Come o'er the waters deep and dark and blue;
> Come where the lilies in the marge have sprung,
> Come with me, love, for Oh, my love is true!"
> This is the song that on the lake was sung,
> The boatman sang it when his heart was young.

Some idea of Whitman's capacity for dramatic narration
may be gained from the following lines taken from "Not
a Man, and Yet a Man," a poem of even greater length
than "The Rape of Florida."

A flash of steely lightning from his hand,
Strikes down the groaning leader of the band;
Divides his startled comrades, and again
Descending, leaves fair Dora's captors slain.
Her, seizing then within a strong embrace,
Out in the dark he wheels his flying pace;

    .   .   .   .   .

He speaks not, but with stalwart tenderness
Her swelling bosom firm to his doth press;
Springs like a stag that flees the eager hound,
And like a whirlwind rustles o'er the ground.
Her locks swim in disheveled wildness o'er
His shoulders, streaming to his waist and more;
While on and on, strong as a rolling flood,
His sweeping footsteps part the silent wood.

It is curious and interesting to trace the growth of individuality and race consciousness in this group of poets. Jupiter Hammon's verses were almost entirely religious exhortations. Only very seldom does Phillis Wheatley sound a native note. Four times in single lines she refers to herself as "Afric's muse." In a poem of admonition addressed to the students at the "University of Cambridge in New England" she refers to herself as follows:

Ye blooming plants of human race divine,
An Ethiop tells you 'tis your greatest foe.

But one looks in vain for some outburst or even complaint against the bondage of her people, for some agonizing cry about her native land. In two poems she refers definitely to Africa as her home, but in each instance there seems to be under the sentiment of the lines a feeling of almost smug contentment at her own escape therefrom. In the poem, "On Being Brought from Africa to America," she says:

> 'Twas mercy brought me from my pagan land,
> Taught my benighted soul to understand
> That there's a God and there's a Saviour too;
> Once I redemption neither sought nor knew.
> Some view our sable race with scornful eye—
> "Their color is a diabolic dye."
> Remember, Christians, Negroes black as Cain,
> May be refined, and join th' angelic train.

In the poem addressed to the Earl of Dartmouth, she speaks of freedom and makes a reference to the parents from whom she was taken as a child, a reference which cannot but strike the reader as rather unimpassioned:

> Should you, my lord, while you peruse my song,
> Wonder from whence my love of Freedom sprung,
> Whence flow these wishes for the common good,
> By feeling hearts alone best understood;
> I, young in life, by seeming cruel fate
> Was snatch'd from Afric's fancy'd happy seat;
> What pangs excruciating must molest,
> What sorrows labor in my parents' breast?
> Steel'd was that soul and by no misery mov'd
> That from a father seiz'd his babe belov'd;
> Such, such my case. And can I then but pray
> Others may never feel tyrannic sway?

The bulk of Phillis Wheatley's work consists of poems addressed to people of prominence. Her book was dedicated to the Countess of Huntington, at whose house she spent the greater part of her time while in England. On his repeal of the Stamp Act, she wrote a poem to King George III, whom she saw later; another poem she wrote to the Earl of Dartmouth, whom she knew. A number of her verses were addressed to other persons of distinction. Indeed, it is apparent that Phillis was far from being a democrat. She was far from being a democrat not only in her social ideas but also in her political ideas; unless a religious meaning is given to the closing lines of her ode to General Washington, she was a decided royalist:

> A crown, a mansion, and a throne that shine
> With gold unfading, Washington! be thine.

Nevertheless, she was an ardent patriot. Her ode to General Washington (1775), her spirited poem, "On Major General Lee" (1776), and her poem, "Liberty and Peace," written in celebration of the close of the war, reveal not only strong patriotic feeling but an understanding of the issues at stake. In her poem, "On Major General Lee," she makes her hero reply thus to the taunts of the British commander into whose hands he has been delivered through treachery:

> O arrogance of tongue!
> And wild ambition, ever prone to wrong!
> Believ'st thou, chief, that armies such as thine
> Can stretch in dust that heaven-defended line?
> In vain allies may swarm from distant lands,
> And demons aid in formidable bands.
> Great as thou art, thou shun'st the field of fame,
> Disgrace to Britain and the British name!
> When offer'd combat by the noble foe
> (Foe to misrule) why did the sword forego
> The easy conquest of the rebel-land?
> Perhaps TOO easy for thy martial hand.

What various causes to the field invite!
For plunder you, and we for freedom fight;
Her cause divine with generous ardor fires,
And every bosom glows as she inspires!
Already thousands of your troops have fled
To the drear mansions of the silent dead:
Columbia, too, beholds with streaming eyes
Her heroes fall—'tis freedom's sacrifice!
So wills the power who with convulsive storms
Shakes impious realms, and nature's face deforms;
Yet those brave troops, innum'rous as the sands,
One soul inspires, one General Chief commands;
Find in your train of boasted heroes, one
To match the praise of Godlike Washington.
Thrice happy Chief in whom the virtues join,
And heaven taught prudence speaks the man divine.

What Phillis Wheatley failed to achieve is due in no small
degree to her education and environment. Her mind was
steeped in the classics; her verses are filled with classical
and mythological allusions. She knew Ovid thoroughly and
was familiar with other Latin authors. She must have known
Alexander Pope by heart. And, too, she was reared and
sheltered in a wealthy and cultured family,—a wealthy and
cultured Boston family; she never had the opportunity to
learn life; she never found out her own true relation to life
and to her surroundings. And it should not be forgotten
that she was only about thirty years old when she died. The
impulsion or the compulsion that might have driven her
genius off the worn paths, out on a journey of exploration,
Phillis Wheatley never received. But, whatever her limita-
tions, she merits more than America has accorded her.

Horton, who was born three years after Phillis Wheat-

ley's death, expressed in all of his poetry strong complaint at
his condition of slavery and a deep longing for freedom.
The following verses are typical of his style and his ability:

> Alas! and am I born for this,
> To wear this slavish chain?
> Deprived of all created bliss,
> Through hardship, toil, and pain?
>
>   .   .   .   .   .
>
> Come, Liberty! thou cheerful sound,
> Roll through my ravished ears;
> Come, let my grief in joys be drowned,
> And drive away my fears.

In Mrs. Harper we find something more than the com-
plaint and the longing of Horton. We find an expression of
a sense of wrong and injustice. The following stanzas are
from a poem addressed to the white women of America:

> You can sigh o'er the sad-eyed Armenian
> Who weeps in her desolate home.
> You can mourn o'er the exile of Russia
> From kindred and friends doomed to roam.
>
>   .   .   .   .   .
>
> But hark! from our Southland are floating
> Sobs of anguish, murmurs of pain;
> And women heart-stricken are weeping
> O'er their tortured and slain.
>
>   .   .   .   .   .
>
> Have ye not, oh, my favored sisters,
> Just a plea, a prayer or a tear
> For mothers who dwell 'neath the shadows
> Of agony, hatred and fear?
>
>   .   .   .   .   .

Weep not, oh, my well sheltered sisters,
   Weep not for the Negro alone,
But weep for your sons who must gather
   The crops which their fathers have sown.

Whitman, in the midst of "The Rape of Florida," a poem in which he related the taking of the State of Florida from the Seminoles, stops and discusses the race question. He discusses it in many other poems; and he discusses it from many different angles. In Whitman we find not only an expression of a sense of wrong and injustice, but we hear a note of faith and a note also of defiance. For example, in the opening to Canto II of "The Rape of Florida":

Greatness by nature cannot be entailed;
It is an office ending with the man,—
Sage, hero, Saviour, tho' the Sire be hailed,
The son may reach obscurity in the van:
Sublime achievements know no patent plan,
Man's immortality's a book with seals,
And none but God shall open—none else can—
But opened, it the mystery reveals,—
Manhood's conquest of man to heaven's respect appeals.

Is manhood less because man's face is black?
Let thunders of the loosened seals reply!
Who shall the rider's restive steed turn back?
Or who withstand the arrows he lets fly
Between the mountains of eternity?
Genius ride forth! Thou gift and torch of heav'n!
The mastery is kindled in thine eye;
To conquest ride! thy bow of strength is giv'n—
The trampled hordes of caste before thee shall be driv'n!

.   .   .   .

'Tis hard to judge if hatred of one's race,
By those who deem themselves superior-born,
Be worse than that quiescence in disgrace,
Which only merits—and should only—scorn.
Oh, let me see the Negro night and morn,
Pressing and fighting in, for place and power!
All earth is place—all time th' auspicious hour,
While heaven leans forth to look, oh, will he quail or cower?

Ah! I abhor his protest and complaint!
His pious looks and patience I despise!
He can't evade the test, disguised as saint;
The manly voice of freedom bids him rise,
And shake himself before Philistine eyes!
And, like a lion roused, no sooner than
A foe dare come, play all his energies,
And court the fray with fury if he can;
For hell itself respects a fearless, manly man.

It may be said that none of these poets strike a deep na-
tive strain or sound a distinctly original note, either in mat-
ter or form. That is true; but the same thing may be said
of all the American poets down to the writers of the present
generation, with the exception of Poe and Walt Whitman.
The thing in which these black poets are mostly excelled by
their contemporaries is mere technique.

Paul Laurence Dunbar stands out as the first poet from
the Negro race in the United States to show a combined
mastery over poetic material and poetic technique, to reveal
innate literary distinction in what he wrote, and to maintain
a high level of performance. He was the first to rise to a
height from which he could take a perspective view of his
own race. He was the first to see objectively its humor, its

superstitions, its shortcomings; the first to feel sympatheti-
cally its heart-wounds, its yearnings, its aspirations, and to
voice them all in a purely literary form.

Dunbar's fame rests chiefly on his poems in Negro dia-
lect. This appraisal of him is, no doubt, fair; for in these
dialect poems he not only carried his art to the highest point
of perfection, but he made a contribution to American litera-
ture unlike what any one else had made, a contribution
which, perhaps, no one else could have made. Of course,
Negro dialect poetry was written before Dunbar wrote, most
of it by white writers; but the fact stands out that Dunbar
was the first to use it as a medium for the true interpretation
of Negro character and psychology. And yet, dialect poetry
does not constitute the whole or even the bulk of Dunbar's
work. In addition to a large number of poems of a very
high order done in literary English, he was the author of
four novels and several volumes of short stories.

Indeed, Dunbar did not begin his career as a writer of
dialect. I may be pardoned for introducing here a bit of
reminiscence. My personal friendship with Paul Dunbar
began before he had achieved recognition, and continued to
be close until his death. When I first met him he had pub-
lished a thin volume, *Oak and Ivy,* which was being sold
chiefly through his own efforts. *Oak and Ivy* showed no dis-
tinctive Negro influence, but rather the influence of James
Whitcomb Riley. At this time Paul and I were together
every day for several months. He talked to me a great deal
about his hopes and ambitions. In these talks he revealed
that he had reached a realization of the possibilities of poetry
in the dialect, together with a recognition of the fact that
it offered the surest way by which he could get a hearing.
Often he said to me: "I've got to write dialect poetry; it's

the only way I can get them to listen to me." I was with Dunbar at the beginning of what proved to be his last illness. He said to me then: "I have not grown. I am writing the same things I wrote ten years ago, and am writing them no better." His self-accusation was not fully true; he had grown, and he had gained a surer control of his art, but he had not accomplished the greater things of which he was constantly dreaming; the public had held him to the things for which it had accorded him recognition. If Dunbar had lived he would have achieved some of those dreams, but even while he talked so dejectedly to me he seemed to feel that he was not to live. He died when he was only thirty-three.

It has a bearing on this entire subject to note that Dunbar was of unmixed Negro blood; so, as the greatest figure in literature which the colored race in the United States has produced, he stands as an example at once refuting and confounding those who wish to believe that whatever extraordinary ability an Aframerican shows is due to an admixture of white blood.

As a man, Dunbar was kind and tender. In conversation he was brilliant and polished. His voice was his chief charm, and was a great element in his success as a reader of his own works. In his actions he was impulsive as a child, sometimes even erratic; indeed, his intimate friends almost looked upon him as a spoiled boy. He was always delicate in health. Temperamentally, he belonged to that class of poets who Taine says are vessels too weak to contain the spirit of poetry, the poets whom poetry kills, the Byrons, the Burnses, the De Mussets, the Poes.

To whom may he be compared, this boy who scribbled his early verses while he ran an elevator, whose youth was a battle against poverty, and who, in spite of almost

insurmountable obstacles, rose to success? A comparison
between him and Burns is not unfitting. The similarity be-
tween many phases of their lives is remarkable, and their
works are not incommensurable. Burns took the strong dia-
lect of his people and made it classic; Dunbar took the
humble speech of his people and in it wrought music.

Mention of Dunbar brings up for consideration the fact
that, although he is the most outstanding figure in litera-
ture among the Aframericans of the United States, he does
not stand alone among the Aframericans of the whole
Western world. There are Plácido and Manzano in Cuba;
Vieux and Durand in Haiti; Machado de Assis in Brazil,
and others still that might be mentioned, who stand on a
plane with or even above Dunbar. Plácido and Machado de
Assis rank as great in the literatures of their respective coun-
tries without any qualifications whatever. They are world
figures in the literature of the Latin languages. Machado de
Assis is somewhat handicapped in this respect by having as
his tongue and medium the lesser known Portuguese, but
Plácido, writing in the language of Spain, Mexico, Cuba
and of almost the whole of South America, is universally
known. His works have been republished in the original in
Spain, Mexico and in most of the Latin-American countries;
several editions have been published in the United States;
translations of his works have been made into French and
German.

Plácido is in some respects the greatest of all the Cuban
poets. In sheer genius and the fire of inspiration he sur-
passes his famous compatriot, Heredia. Then, too, his birth,
his life and his death ideally contained the tragic elements
that go into the making of a halo about a poet's head.
Plácido was born in Habana in 1809. The first months of

his life were passed in a foundling asylum; indeed, his real name, Gabriel de la Concepcion Valdés, was in honor of its founder. His father took him out of the asylum, but shortly afterwards went to Mexico and died there. His early life was a struggle against poverty; his youth and manhood was a struggle for Cuban independence. His death placed him in the list of Cuban martyrs. On the twenty-seventh of June, 1844, he was lined up against a wall with ten others and shot by order of the Spanish authorities on a charge of conspiracy. In his short but eventful life he turned out work which bulks more than six hundred pages. During the few hours preceding his execution he wrote three of his best-known poems, among them his famous sonnet, "Mother, Farewell!"

Plácido's sonnet to his mother has been translated into every important language; William Cullen Bryant did it in English; but in spite of its wide popularity, it is, perhaps, outside of Cuba the least understood of all Plácido's poems. It is curious to note how Bryant's translation totally misses the intimate sense of the delicate subtility of the poem. The American poet makes it a tender and loving farewell of a son who is about to die to a heart-broken mother; but that is not the kind of a farewell that Plácido intended to write or did write.

The key to the poem is in the first word, and the first word is the Spanish conjunction *Si* (if). The central idea, then, of the sonnet is, "If the sad fate which now overwhelms me should bring a pang to your heart, do not weep, for I die a glorious death and sound the last note of my lyre to you." Bryant either failed to understand or ignored the opening word, "If," because he was not familiar with the poet's history.

While Plácido's father was a Negro, his mother was a
Spanish white woman, a dancer in one of the Habana
theaters. At his birth she abandoned him to a foundling
asylum, and perhaps never saw him again, although it is
known that she outlived her son. When the poet came down
to his last hours he remembered that somewhere there lived
a woman who was his mother; that although she had heart-
lessly abandoned him; that although he owed her no filial
duty, still she might, perhaps, on hearing of his sad end feel
some pang of grief or sadness; so he tells her in his last
words that he dies happy and bids her not to weep. This he
does with nobility and dignity, but absolutely without affec-
tion. Taking into account these facts, and especially their
humiliating and embittering effect upon a soul so sensitive
as Placido's, this sonnet, in spite of the obvious weakness
of the sestet as compared with the octave, is a remarkable
piece of work.[1]

In considering the Aframerican poets of the Latin lan-
guages I am impelled to think that, as up to this time the
colored poets of greater universality have come out of the
Latin-American countries rather than out of the United
States, they will continue to do so for a good many years.
The reason for this I hinted at in the first part of this
preface. The colored poet in the United States labors within
limitations which he cannot easily pass over. He is always
on the defensive or the offensive. The pressure upon him to
be propagandic is well nigh irresistible. These conditions are
suffocating to breadth and to real art in poetry. In addition
he labors under the handicap of finding culture not entirely
colorless in the United States. On the other hand, the colored

[1] Plácido's sonnet and two English versions will be found in the
Appendix.

poet of Latin America can voice the national spirit without any reservations. And he will be rewarded without any reservations, whether it be to place him among the great or declare him the greatest.

So I think it probable that the first world-acknowledged Aframerican poet will come out of Latin America. Over against this probability, of course, is the great advantage possessed by the colored poet in the United States of writing in the world-conquering English language.

This preface has gone far beyond what I had in mind when I started. It was my intention to gather together the best verses I could find by Negro poets and present them with a bare word of introduction. It was not my plan to make this collection inclusive nor to make the book in any sense a book of criticism. I planned to present only verses by contemporary writers; but, perhaps, because this is the first collection of its kind, I realized the absence of a starting-point and was led to provide one and to fill in with historical data what I felt to be a gap.

It may be surprising to many to see how little of the poetry being written by Negro poets today is being written in Negro dialect. The newer Negro poets show a tendency to discard dialect; much of the subject-matter which went into the making of traditional dialect poetry, 'possums, watermelons, etc., they have discarded altogether, at least, as poetic material. This tendency will, no doubt, be regretted by the majority of white readers; and, indeed, it would be a distinct loss if the American Negro poets threw away this quaint and musical folk speech as a medium of expression. And yet, after all, these poets are working through a problem not realized by the reader, and, perhaps, by many of

these poets themselves not realized consciously. They are try-
ing to break away from, not Negro dialect itself, but the
limitations on Negro dialect imposed by the fixing effects
of long convention.

The Negro in the United States has achieved or been
placed in a certain artistic niche. When he is thought of
artistically, it is as a happy-go-lucky, singing, shuffling,
banjo-picking being or as a more or less pathetic figure. The
picture of him is in a log cabin amid fields of cotton or
along the levees. Negro dialect is naturally and by long asso-
ciation the exact instrument for voicing this phase of Negro
life; and by that very exactness it is an instrument with but
two full stops, humor and pathos. So even when he confines
himself to purely racial themes, the Aframerican poet real-
izes that there are phases of Negro life in the United States
which cannot be treated in the dialect either adequately or
artistically. Take, for example, the phases rising out of life
in Harlem, that most wonderful Negro city in the world.
I do not deny that a Negro in a log cabin is more picturesque
than a Negro in a Harlem flat, but the Negro in the Harlem
flat is here, and he is but part of a group growing every-
where in the country, a group whose ideals are becoming
increasingly more vital than those of the traditionally artistic
group, even if its members are less picturesque.

What the colored poet in the United States needs to do is
something like what Synge did for the Irish; he needs to
find a form that will express the racial spirit by symbols from
within rather than by symbols from without, such as the
mere mutilation of English spelling and pronunciation. He
needs a form that is freer and larger than dialect, but which
will still hold the racial flavor; a form expressing the
imagery, the idioms, the peculiar turns of thought, and the

distinctive humor and pathos, too, of the Negro, but which will also be capable of voicing the deepest and highest emotions and aspirations, and allow of the widest range of subjects and the widest scope of treatment.

Negro dialect is at present a medium that is not capable of giving expression to the varied conditions of Negro life in America, and much less is it capable of giving the fullest interpretation of Negro character and psychology. This is no indictment against the dialect as dialect, but against the mold of convention in which Negro dialect in the United States has been set. In time these conventions may become lost, and the colored poet in the United States may sit down to write in dialect without feeling that his first line will put the general reader in a frame of mind which demands that the poem be humorous or pathetic. In the meantime, there is no reason why these poets should not continue to do the beautiful things that can be done, and done best, in the dialect.

In stating the need for Aframerican poets in the United States to work out a new and distinctive form of expression I do not wish to be understood to hold any theory that they should limit themselves to Negro poetry, to racial themes; the sooner they are able to write *American* poetry spontaneously, the better. Nevertheless, I believe that the richest contribution the Negro poet can make to the American literature of the future will be the fusion into it of his own individual artistic gifts.

Not many of the writers here included, except Dunbar, are known at all to the general reading public; and there is only one of these who has a widely recognized position in the American literary world, William Stanley Braithwaite.

Mr. Braithwaite is not only unique in this respect, but he stands unique among all the Aframerican writers the United States has yet produced. He has gained his place, taking as the standard and measure for his work the identical standard and measure applied to American writers and American literature. He has asked for no allowances or rewards, either directly or indirectly, on account of his race.

Mr. Braithwaite is the author of two volumes of verses, lyrics of delicate and tenuous beauty. In his more recent and uncollected poems he shows himself more and more decidedly the mystic. But his place in American literature is due more to his work as a critic and anthologist than to his work as a poet. There is still another rôle he has played, that of friend of poetry and poets. It is a recognized fact that in the work which preceded the present revival of poetry in the United States, no one rendered more unremitting and valuable service than Mr. Braithwaite. And it can be said that no future study of American poetry of this age can be made without reference to Braithwaite.

Two authors included in the book are better known for their work in prose than in poetry: W. E. B. Du Bois whose well-known prose at its best is, however, impassioned and rhythmical; and Benjamin Brawley who is the author, among other works, of one of the best handbooks on the English drama that has yet appeared in America.

But the group of the new Negro poets, whose work makes up the bulk of this anthology, contains names destined to be known. Claude McKay, although still quite a young man, has already demonstrated his power, breadth and skill as a poet. Mr. McKay's breadth is as essential a part of his equipment as his power and skill. He demonstrates mastery of the three when as a Negro poet he pours out the bitterness and rebellion in his heart in those two sonnet-tragedies, "If We Must Die" and "To the White Fiends," in a manner that strikes terror; and when as a cosmic poet he creates the atmosphere and mood of poetic beauty in the absolute, as he does in "Spring in New Hampshire" and "The Harlem Dancer." Mr. McKay gives evidence that he has passed beyond the danger which threatens many of the new Negro poets—the danger of allowing the purely polemical phases of the race problem to choke their sense of artistry.

Mr. McKay's earliest work is unknown in this country. It consists of poems written and published in his native Jamaica. I was fortunate enough to run across this first volume, and I could not refrain from reproducing here one of the poems written in the West Indian Negro dialect. I have done this not only to illustrate the widest range of the poet's talent and to offer a comparison between the American and the West Indian dialects, but on account of the intrinsic worth of the poem itself. I was much tempted to introduce several more, in spite of the fact that they might require a glossary, because however greater work Mr. McKay may do he can never do anything more touching and charming than these poems in the Jamaica dialect.

Fenton Johnson is a young poet of the ultra-modern school who gives promise of greater work than he has yet done. Jessie Fauset shows that she possesses the lyric gift, and she works with care and finish. Miss Fauset is especially adept in her translations from the French. Georgia Douglas Johnson is a poet neither afraid nor ashamed of her emotions. She limits herself to the purely conventional forms, rhythms and rhymes, but through them she achieves striking effects. The principal theme of Mrs. Johnson's poems is the secret dread down in every woman's heart, the dread of the passing of youth and beauty, and with them love. An old theme, one which poets themselves have often wearied of, but which, like death, remains one of the imperishable themes on which is made the poetry that has moved men's hearts through all ages. In her ingenuously wrought verses, through sheer simplicity and spontaneousness, Mrs. Johnson often sounds a note of pathos or passion that will not fail to waken a response, except in those too sophisticated or cynical to respond to natural impulses. Of the half dozen or so colored women writing creditable verse, Anne Spencer is the most modern and least obvious in her methods. Her lines are at times involved and turgid and almost cryptic, but she shows an originality which does not depend upon eccentricities. In her "Before the Feast of Shushan" she displays an opulence, the love of which has long been charged against the Negro as one of his naïve and childish traits, but which in art may infuse a much needed color, warmth and spirit of abandon into American poetry.

John W. Holloway, more than any Negro poet writing in the dialect today, summons to his work the lilt, the spontaneity and charm of which Dunbar was the supreme master whenever he employed that medium. It is well to say a word here about the dialect poems of James Edwin Campbell. In dialect, Campbell was a precursor of Dunbar. A comparison of his idioms and phonetics with those of Dunbar reveals great differences. Dunbar is a shade or two more sophisticated and his phonetics approach nearer to a mean standard of the dialects spoken in the different sections. Campbell is more primitive and his phonetics are those of the dialect as spoken by the Negroes of the sea islands off the coasts of South Carolina and Georgia, which to this day remains comparatively close to its African roots, and is strik-

ingly similar to the speech of the uneducated Negroes of the
West Indies. An error that confuses many persons in read-
ing or understanding Negro dialect is the idea that it is uni-
form. An ignorant Negro of the uplands of Georgia would
have almost as much difficulty in understanding an ignorant
sea island Negro as an Englishman would have. Not even
in the dialect of any particular section is a given word always
pronounced in precisely the same way. Its pronunciation de-
pends upon the preceding and following sounds. Sometimes
the combination permits of a liaison so close that to the
uninitiated the sound of the word is almost completely lost.

The constant effort in Negro dialect is to elide all trouble-
some consonants and sounds. This negative effort may be
after all only positive laziness of the vocal organs, but the
result is a softening and smoothing which makes Negro dia-
lect so delightfully easy for singers.

Daniel Webster Davis wrote dialect poetry at the time
when Dunbar was writing. He gained great popularity, but
it did not spread beyond his own race. Davis had unctuous
humor, but he was crude. For illustration, note the vast
stretch between his "Hog Meat" and Dunbar's "When de
Co'n Pone's Hot," both of them poems on the traditional
ecstasy of the Negro in contemplation of "good things"
to eat.

It is regrettable that two of the most gifted writers in-
cluded were cut off so early in life. R. C. Jamison and
Joseph S. Cotter, Jr., died several years ago, both of them in
their youth. Jamison was barely thirty at the time of his
death, but among his poems there is one, at least, which
stamps him as a poet of superior talent and lofty inspiration.
"The Negro Soldiers" is a poem with the race problem as its
theme, yet it transcends the limits of race and rises to a

spiritual height that makes it one of the noblest poems of the Great War. Cotter died a mere boy of twenty, and the latter part of that brief period he passed in an invalid state. Some months before his death he published a thin volume of verses which were for the most part written on a sick bed. In this little volume Cotter showed fine poetic sense and a free and bold mastery over his material. A reading of Cotter's poems is certain to induce that mood in which one will regretfully speculate on what the young poet might have accomplished had he not been cut off so soon.

As intimated above, my original idea for this book underwent a change in the writing of the introduction. I first planned to select twenty-five to thirty poems which I judged to be up to a certain standard, and offer them with a few words of introduction and without comment. In the collection, as it grew to be, that "certain standard" has been broadened if not lowered; but I believe that this is offset by the advantage of the wider range given the reader and the student of the subject.

I offer this collection without making apology or asking allowance. I feel confident that the reader will find not only an earnest for the future, but actual achievement. The reader cannot but be impressed by the distance already covered. It is a long way from the plaints of George Horton to the invectives of Claude McKay, from the obviousness of Frances Harper to the complexness of Anne Spencer. Much ground has been covered, but more will yet be covered. It is this side of prophecy to declare that the undeniable creative genius of the Negro is destined to make a distinctive and valuable contribution to American poetry.

I wish to extend my thanks to Mr. Arthur A. Schomburg, who placed his valuable collection of books by Negro authors at my disposal. I wish also to acknowledge with thanks the kindness of Dodd, Mead and Company for permitting the reprint of poems by Paul Laurence Dunbar; of the Cornhill Publishing Company for permission to reprint poems of Georgia Douglas Johnson, Joseph S. Cotter, Jr., and Bertram Johnson; and of Neale & Co. for permission to reprint poems of John W. Holloway. I wish to thank Mr. Braithwaite for permission to use the included poems from his forthcoming volume, *Sandy Star and Willie Gee.* And to acknowledge the courtesy of the following magazines: *The Crisis, The Century Magazine, The Liberator, The Freeman, The Independent, Others,* and *Poetry: A Magazine of Verse.*

JAMES WELDON JOHNSON

New York City
1921

PAUL LAURENCE DUNBAR

PAUL LAURENCE DUNBAR *was born at Dayton, Ohio, June 27, 1872, the son of former slaves. He attended the public schools of that city and was graduated from the high school in 1891. He began writing verse during his grammar school days. Some of his early poems he wrote while earning a living by running a passenger elevator in a Dayton building. His first volume of poems,* Oak and Ivy, *was published in 1893, and was sold chiefly through his own efforts. A second volume,* Majors and Minors, *of which he was also chief salesman, appeared in January, 1895. A very favorable review of this book by William Dean Howells attracted attention to the poems and the poet, and made possible the bringing out of a third volume,* Lyrics of Lowly Life, *under the imprint of Dodd, Mead and Company, New York. This third volume, with an introduction by Howells, gained instant national recognition for Dunbar.* Lyrics of Lowly Life *(1896) was followed by* Lyrics of the Hearthside *(1899),* Lyrics of Love and Laughter *(1903), and* Lyrics of Sunshine and Shadow *(1905). From the poems in these volumes several editions of illustrated poems were culled and printed. In 1899, influential friends secured for him an appointment to a position in the Congressional Library; but the job irked him, and he gave it up. The edition of Dunbar's collected poems was brought out in 1918. A number of his lyrics have been set to music by well-known composers.*

There have been many changes in the estimates of

Negro poetry since Dunbar died (February 9, 1906), but he still holds his place as the first American Negro poet of real literary distinction. There are some who will differ with this statement, feeling that it should be made about Phillis Wheatley. It is true that Phillis Wheatley did measure up to the best of her contemporaries; but it must be remembered that not one of her contemporaries was a poet of real literary distinction. Dunbar was the first to demonstrate a high degree of poetic talent combined with literary training and technical proficiency. In the field in which he became best known, Negro dialect poetry, his work has not been excelled.

Dunbar's fame rests almost wholly upon his Negro dialect poetry. He was not the first, however, to write Negro dialect poems, nor did he himself begin by writing in Negro dialect. Irwin Russell (1853-'79), a white poet, was perhaps the first to use the dialect in a literary verse form. A glance at his work will reveal how much Dunbar is indebted to him; it will also reveal that Dunbar surpasses him. Dunbar's earliest verses show the influence of James Whitcomb Riley, and were patterned after Riley's Hoosier dialect poetry. This influence persisted even after Dunbar began writing in Negro dialect, but it did not limit him. It is interesting to compare Dunbar's "When De Co'n Pone's Hot" with Riley's "When the Frost Is on the Punkin," and note the similarity of sentiment and the nearly identical rhythmic structure. It is also interesting to note how Dunbar demonstrates a defter technique and a more delicate sense in handling the nuances of sentiment than his early master. He gives "When De Co'n Pone's Hot" a more musical lilt, and reduces metrical monotony by compressing his stanza into what is actually a verse scheme of six couplets. And by this line arrangement he gives to the recurring title line a cumu-

lative force that Riley misses giving to the title line of "When the Frost Is on the Punkin." Dunbar profited by Riley's influence, and he transcended it.

Dunbar made Negro dialect poetry popular and so founded a school. He was imitated by many writers, both white and colored, none of whom quite equaled him in humor, tenderness, and charm, and in the finish with which he generally worked. He was also the author of many poems done in literary English, a number of which are of very high order. "Ere Sleep Comes Down to Soothe the Weary Eyes" is by all the tests one among the finest poems in American literature. It possesses moving sincerity, passion, and beauty; it carries finality, and is done with faultless workmanship. And it does not stand entirely unmatched among his poems in literary English. Partly because of his magnificent voice, he was a very successful reader of his own poetry and was in this way able to add greatly to its popularity.

Much of the poetry on which Dunbar's fame rests has passed; just as much of the poetry of his even more popular contemporary, Riley, has passed. Dialect poetry still holds a place in American literature, but the place itself is no longer considered an important one. The qualities that gave it vogue—tenderness, sentimentality, homely humor, genial optimism—are the very qualities that now bring disparagement upon it. Dunbar wrought delightful music in the dialect and gained the national ear; but, perhaps, after all, the final estimate of him will rest upon those poems in literary English in which he sincerely and courageously voiced his own people, together with those in which he achieved the universal note—probably a judgment he would have desired most.

In addition to poetical works, Dunbar was the author of

four novels, The Uncalled, The Love of Landry, The Sport
of the Gods, *and* The Fanatics. *He was a frequent contrib-
utor of short stories to the magazines; and these were col-
lected and published in several volumes.*

A NEGRO LOVE SONG[1]

Seen my lady home las' night,
   Jump back, honey, jump back.
Hel' huh han' an' sque'z it tight,
   Jump back, honey, jump back.
Hyeahd huh sigh a little sigh,
Seen a light gleam f'om huh eye,
An' a smile go flittin' by—
   Jump back, honey, jump back.

Hyeahd de win' blow thoo de pine,
   Jump back, honey, jump back.
Mockin'-bird was singin' fine,
   Jump back, honey, jump back.
An' my hea't was beatin' so,
When I reached my lady's do',
Dat I could n't ba' to go—
   Jump back, honey, jump back.

Put my ahm aroun' huh wais',
   Jump back, honey, jump back.
Raised huh lips an' took a tase,
   Jump back, honey, jump back.
Love me, honey, love me true?
Love me well ez I love you?

[1] Copyright by Dodd, Mead & Company.

An' she answe'd, "Cose I do"—
   Jump back, honey, jump back.

LITTLE BROWN BABY

Little brown baby wif spa'klin' eyes,
   Come to yo' pappy an' set on his knee.
What you been doin', suh—makin' san' pies?
   Look at dat bib—You's ez du'ty ez me.
Look at dat mouf—dat's merlasses, I bet;
   Come hyeah, Maria, an' wipe off his han's.
Bees gwine to ketch you an' eat you up yit,
   Bein' so sticky an' sweet—goodness lan's!

Little brown baby wif spa'klin' eyes,
   Who's pappy's darlin' an' who's pappy's chile?
Who is it all de day nevah once tries
   Fu' to be cross, er once loses dat smile?
Whah did you git dem teef? My, you's a scamp!
   Whah did dat dimple come f'om in yo' chin?
Pappy do' know you—I b'lieves you's a tramp;
   Mammy, dis hyeah's some ol' straggler got in!

Let's th'ow him outen de do' in de san',
   We do' want stragglers a-layin' 'roun' hyeah;
Let's gin him 'way to de big buggah-man;
   I know he's hidin' erroun' hyeah right neah.
Buggah-man, buggah-man, come in de do',
   Hyeah's a bad boy you kin have fu' to eat.
Mammy an' pappy do' want him no mo',
   Swaller him down f'om his haid to his feet!

Dah, now, I t'ought dat you'd hug me up close.
  Go back, ol' buggah, you sha'n't have dis boy.
He ain't no tramp, ner no straggler, of co'se;
  He's pappy's pa'dner an' playmate an' joy.
Come to you' pallet now—go to you' res';
  Wisht you could allus know ease an' cleah skies;
Wisht you could stay jes' a chile on my breas'—
  Little brown baby wif spa'klin' eyes!

ERE SLEEP COMES DOWN TO SOOTHE THE WEARY EYES

Ere sleep comes down to soothe the weary eyes,
Which all the day with ceaseless care have sought
The magic gold which from the seeker flies;
Ere dreams put on the gown and cap of thought,
And make the waking world a world of lies,—
Of lies most palpable, uncouth, forlorn,
That say life's full of aches and tears and sighs—
Oh, how with more than dreams the soul is torn,
Ere sleep comes down to soothe the weary eyes.

Ere sleep comes down to soothe the weary eyes,
How all the griefs and heartaches we have known
Come up like pois'nous vapors that arise
From some base witch's caldron, when the crone,
To work some potent spell, her magic plies.
The past which held its share of bitter pain,
Whose ghost we prayed that Time might exorcise,
Comes up, is lived and suffered o'er again,
Ere sleep comes down to soothe the weary eyes.

Ere sleep comes down to soothe the weary eyes,
What phantoms fill the dimly lighted room;
What ghostly shades in awe-creating guise
Are bodied forth within the teeming gloom.
What echoes faint of sad and soul-sick cries,
And pangs of vague inexplicable pain
That pay the spirit's ceaseless enterprise,
Come thronging through the chambers of the brain,
Ere sleep comes down to soothe the weary eyes.

Ere sleep comes down to soothe the weary eyes,
Where ranges forth the spirit far and free?
Through what strange realms and unfamiliar skies
Tends her far course to lands of mystery?
To lands unspeakable—beyond surmise,
Where shapes unknowable to being spring,
Till, faint of wing, the Fancy fails and dies
Much wearied with the spirit's journeying,
Ere sleep comes down to soothe the weary eyes.

Ere sleep comes down to soothe the weary eyes,
How questioneth the soul that other soul—
The inner sense which neither cheats nor lies,
But self exposes unto self, a scroll
Full writ with all life's acts unwise or wise,
In characters indelible and known;
So, trembling with the shock of sad surprise,
The soul doth view its awful self alone,
Ere sleep comes down to soothe the weary eyes.

When sleep comes down to seal the weary eyes,
The last dear sleep whose soft embrace is balm,

And whom sad sorrow teaches us to prize
For kissing all our passions into calm,
Ah, then, no more we heed the sad world's cries,
Or seek to probe th' eternal mystery,
Or fret our souls at long-withheld replies,
At glooms through which our visions cannot see,
When sleep comes down to seal the weary eyes.

SHIPS THAT PASS IN THE NIGHT

Out in the sky the great dark clouds are massing;
   I look far out into the pregnant night,
Where I can hear a solemn booming gun
   And catch the gleaming of a random light,
That tells me that the ship I seek is passing, passing.

My tearful eyes my soul's deep hurt are glassing;
   For I would hail and check that ship of ships.
I stretch my hands imploring, cry aloud,
   My voice falls dead a foot from mine own lips,
And but its ghost doth reach that vessel, passing, passing.

O Earth, O Sky, O Ocean, both surpassing,
   O heart of mine, O soul that dreads the dark!
Is there no hope for me? Is there no way
   That I may sight and check that speeding bark
Which out of sight and sound is passing, passing?

LOVER'S LANE

   Summah night an' sighin' breeze,
     'Long de lovah's lane;

Frien'ly, shadder-mekin' trees,
    'Long de lovah's lane.
White folks' wo'k all done up gran'—
Me an' 'Mandy han'-in-han'
Struttin' lak we owned de lan',
    'Long de lovah's lane.

Owl a-settin' 'side de road,
    'Long de lovah's lane,
Lookin' at us lak he knowed
    Dis uz lovah's lane.
Go on, hoot yo' mou'nful tune,
You ain' nevah loved in June,
An' come hidin' f'om de moon
    Down in lovah's lane.

Bush it ben' an' nod an' sway,
    Down in lovah's lane,
Try'n' to hyeah me whut I say
    'Long de lovah's lane.
But I whispahs low lak dis,
An' my 'Mandy smile huh bliss—
Mistah Bush he shek his fis',
    Down in lovah's lane.

Whut I keer ef day is long,
    Down in lovah's lane.
I kin allus sing a song
    'Long de lovah's lane.
An' de wo'ds I hyeah an' say
Meks up fu' de weary day
W'en I's strollin' by de way,
    Down in lovah's lane.

An' dis t'ought will allus rise
　　Down in lovah's lane;
Wondah whethah in de skies
　　Dey's a lovah's lane.
Ef dey ain't, I tell you true,
'Ligion do look mighty blue,
'Cause I do' know whut I'd do
　　'Dout a lovah's lane.

THE DEBT

This is the debt I pay
Just for one riotous day,
　Years of regret and grief,
Sorrow without relief.

Pay it I will to the end—
Until the grave, my friend,
Gives me a true release—
Gives me the clasp of peace.

Slight was the thing I bought,
Small was the debt I thought,
Poor was the loan at best—
God! but the interest!

THE HAUNTED OAK

Pray why are you so bare, so bare,
　Oh, bough of the old oak-tree;
And why, when I go through the shade you throw,
　Runs a shudder over me?

My leaves were green as the best, I trow,
   And sap ran free in my veins,
But I saw in the moonlight dim and weird
   A guiltless victim's pains.

I bent me down to hear his sigh;
   I shook with his gurgling moan,
And I trembled sore when they rode away,
   And left him here alone.

They'd charged him with the old, old crime,
   And set him fast in jail:
Oh, why does the dog howl all night long,
   And why does the night wind wail?

He prayed his prayer and he swore his oath,
   And he raised his hand to the sky;
But the beat of hoofs smote on his ear,
   And the steady tread drew nigh.

Who is it rides by night, by night,
   Over the moonlit road?
And what is the spur that keeps the pace,
   What is the galling goad?

And now they beat at the prison door,
   "Ho, keeper, do not stay!
We are friends of him whom you hold within,
   And we fain would take him away

"From those who ride fast on our heels
   With mind to do him wrong;
They have no care for his innocence,
   And the rope they bear is long."

They have fooled the jailer with lying words,
  They have fooled the man with lies;
The bolts unbar, the locks are drawn,
  And the great door open flies.

Now they have taken him from the jail,
  And hard and fast they ride,
And the leader laughs low down in his throat,
  As they halt my trunk beside.

Oh, the judge, he wore a mask of black,
  And the doctor one of white,
And the minister, with his oldest son,
  Was curiously bedight.

Oh, foolish man, why weep you now?
  'Tis but a little space,
And the time will come when these shall dread
  The mem'ry of your face.

I feel the rope against my bark,
  And the weight of him in my grain,
I feel in the throe of his final woe
  The touch of my own last pain.

And never more shall leaves come forth
  On a bough that bears the ban;
I am burned with dread, I am dried and dead,
  From the curse of a guiltless man.

And ever the judge rides by, rides by,
  And goes to hunt the deer,
And ever another rides his soul
  In the guise of a mortal fear.

And ever the man he rides me hard,
   And never a night stays he;
For I feel his curse as a haunted bough
   On the trunk of a haunted tree.

WHEN DE CO'N PONE'S HOT

Dey is times in life when Nature
   Seems to slip a cog an' go,
Jes' a-rattlin' down creation,
   Lak an ocean's overflow;
When de worl' jes' stahts a-spinnin'
   Lak a picaninny's top,
An' yo' cup o' joy is brimmin'
   'Twell it seems about to slop,
An' you feel jes' lak a racah,
   Dat is trainin' fu' to trot—
When yo' mammy says de blessin'
   An' de co'n pone's hot.

When you set down at de table,
   Kin' o' weary lak an' sad,
An' you'se jes' a little tiahed
   An' purhaps a little mad;
How yo' gloom tu'ns into gladness,
   How yo' joy drives out de doubt
When de oven do' is opened,
   An' de smell comes po'in' out;
Why, de 'lectric light o' Heaven
   Seems to settle on de spot,
When yo' mammy says de blessin'
   An' de co'n pone's hot.

When de cabbage pot is steamin'
   An' de bacon good an' fat,
When de chittlins is a-sputter'n'
   So's to show you whah dey's at;
Tek away yo' sody biscuit,
   Tek away yo' cake an' pie,
Fu' de glory time is comin',
   An' it's 'proachin' mighty nigh,
An' you want to jump an' hollah,
   Dough you know you'd bettah not,
When yo' mammy says de blessin'
   An' de co'n pone's hot.

I have hyeahd o' lots o' sermons,
   An' I've hyeahd o' lots o' prayers,
An' I've listened to some singin'
   Dat has tuck me up de stairs
Of de Glory-Lan' an' set me
   Jes' below de Mastah's th'one,
An' have lef' my hea't a-singin'
   In a happy aftah tone;
But dem wu'ds so sweetly murmured
   Seem to tech de softes' spot,
When my mammy says de blessin',
   An' de co'n pone's hot.

A DEATH SONG

Lay me down beneaf de willers in de grass,
Whah de branch'll go a-singin' as it pass.
   An' w'en I's a-layin' low,
   I kin hyeah it as it go
Singin', "Sleep, my honey, tek yo' res' at las'."

Lay me nigh to whah hit meks a little pool,
An' de watah stan's so quiet lak an' cool,
 Whah de little birds in spring,
 Ust to come an' drink an' sing,
An' de chillen waded on dey way to school.

Let me settle w'en my shouldahs draps dey load
Nigh enough to hyeah de noises in de road;
 Fu' I t'ink de las' long res'
 Gwine to soothe my sperrit bes'
If I's layin' 'mong de t'ings I's allus knowed.

JAMES EDWIN CAMPBELL

JAMES EDWIN CAMPBELL *was born at Pomeroy, Ohio, in the early '60's. Little or nothing is known of his youth; he never referred to it even among his closest associates. He was educated in the public schools of his native town, and spent a while at Miami College. In the late '80's and early '90's he was engaged in newspaper work in Chicago. He wrote regularly on various dailies of that city. He was also one of a group that issued the* Four O'Clock Magazine, *a literary publication that flourished for several years. He was the author of* Echoes from the Cabin and Elsewhere, *a volume of poems.*

Campbell preceded Dunbar as a writer of Negro dialect poetry. Indeed, it appears that he was the first Aframerican poet to work in the dialect. However, he did not, it seems, have any influence on Dunbar, who follows in a line from Irwin Russell. Nevertheless, it is quite probable that Dunbar knew Campbell, as there was one period when both poets lived in Chicago. Campbell, in his idioms and phonetics, is wholly distinct from both Russell and Dunbar. His dialect, idiomatically and phonetically, is nearer to the Gullah or to the West Indian dialect. His use of the broad "a" and of the objective form of the personal pronouns for the nominative is not in accord with the pronunciation and mode of speech used generally by the Negro in the United States for, at least, the past half century. There is more than a slight similarity between his earlier poems and the poems of Claude McKay in the West Indian dialect.

In some of his later poems Campbell seems to have felt the

64

Dunbar influence, but at no point does he equal Dunbar in workmanship. Yet it should be said for him that relatively he was free from the "sweetness" of the plantation tradition. His tone is generally firm. He also attempted poetry in literary English, but without any marked success. His poem "Compensation" has a theme for genuine poetry, and it starts well, but the latter half trails off into mere echoes of poetry, even to "laverocks" and "gorse" and "heather." Campbell died twenty-five or so years ago.

NEGRO SERENADE

O, de light-bugs glimmer down de lane,
    Merlindy! Merlindy!
O, de whip'-will callin' notes ur pain—
    Merlindy, O, Merlindy!
O, honey lub, my turkle dub,
    Doan' you hyuh my bawnjer ringin',
While de night-dew falls an' de ho'n owl calls
    By de ol' ba'n gate Ise singin'.

O, Miss 'Lindy, doan' you hyuh me, chil',
    Merlindy! Merlindy!
My lub fur you des dribe me wil'—
    Merlindy, O, Merlindy!
I'll sing dis night twel broad day-light,
    Ur bu's' my froat wid tryin',
'Less you come down, Miss 'Lindy Brown,
    An' stops dis ha't f'um sighin'!

DE CUNJAH MAN

O chillen, run, de Cunjah man,
    Him mouf ez beeg ez fryin' pan,

Him yurs am small, him eyes am raid,
Him hab no toof een him ol' haid,
Him hab him roots, him wu'k him trick,
Him roll him eye, him mek you sick—
    De Cunjah man, de Cunjah man,
    O chillen, run, de Cunjah man!

Him hab ur ball ob raid, raid ha'r,
Him hide it un' de kitchen sta'r,
Mam Jude huh pars urlong dat way,
An' now huh hab ur snaik, de say.
Him wrop ur roun' huh buddy tight,
Huh eyes pop out, ur orful sight—
    De Cunjah man, de Cunjah man,
    O chillen, run, de Cunjah man!

Miss Jane, huh dribe him f'um huh do',
An' now huh hens woan' lay no mo';
De Jussey cow huh done fall sick,
Hit all done by de Cunjah trick.
Him put ur root un' 'Lijah's baid,
An' now de man he sho' am daid—
    De Cunjah man, de Cunjah man,
    O chillen, run, de Cunjah man!

Me see him stan' de yudder night
Right een de road een white moon-light;
Him toss him arms, him whirl him 'roun',
Him stomp him foot urpon de groun';
De snaiks come crawlin', one by one,
Me hyuh um hiss, me break an' run—
    De Cunjah man, de Cunjah man,
    O chillen, run, de Cunjah man!

UNCLE EPH'S BANJO SONG

Clean de ba'n an' sweep de flo',
    Sing, my bawnjer, sing!
We's gwine ter dawnce dis eb'nin' sho',
    Ring, my bawnjer, ring!
Den hits up de road an' down de lane,
Hurry, niggah, you miss de train;
De yaller gal she dawnce so neat,
De yaller gal she look so sweet,
    Ring, my bawnjer, ring!

De moon come up, de sun go down,
    Sing, my bawnjer, sing!
De niggahs am all come f'um town,
    Ring, my bawnjer, ring!
Den hits roun' de hill an' froo de fiel'—
Lookout dar, niggah, doan' you steal!
De milyuns on dem vines am green,
De moon am bright, O you'll be seen,
    Ring, my bawnjer, ring!

OL' DOC' HYAR

Ur ol' Hyar lib in ur house on de hill,
He hunner yurs ol' an' nebber wuz ill;
He yurs dee so long an' he eyes so beeg,
An' he laigs so spry dat he dawnce ur jeeg;
He lib so long dat he know ebbry tings
'Bout de beas'ses dat walks an' de bu'ds dat sings—
                Dis Ol' Doc' Hyar,
                Whar lib up dar
Een ur mighty fine house on ur mighty high hill.

He doctah fur all de beas'ses an' bu'ds—
He put on he specs an' he use beeg wu'ds,
He feel dee pu's 'den he look mighty wise,
He pull out he watch an' he shet bofe eyes;
He grab up he hat an' grab up he cane,
Den—"blam!" go de do'—he gone lak de train,
                         Dis Ol' Doc' Hyar,
                         Whar lib up dar
Een ur mighty fine house on ur mighty high hill.

Mistah Ba'r fall sick—dee sont fur Doc' Hyar,
"Oh, Doctah, come queeck, an' see Mr. Ba'r;
He mighty nigh daid des sho' ez you bo'n!
Too much ur young peeg, too much ur green co'n,"
Ez he put on he hat, said Ol' Doc' Hyar;
"I'll tek 'long meh lawnce, an' lawnce Mistah B'ar,"
                         Said Ol' Doc' Hyar,
                         Whar lib up dar
Een ur mighty fine house on ur mighty high hill.

Mistah B'ar he groaned, Mistah B'ar he growled,
W'ile de ol' Miss B'ar an' de chillen howled;
Doctah Hyar tuk out he sha'p li'l lawnce,
An' pyu'ced Mistah B'ar twel he med him prawnce
Den grab up he hat an' grab up he cane
"Blam!" go de do' an' he gone lak de train,
                         Dis Ol' Doc' Hyar,
                         Whar lib up dar
Een ur mighty fine house on ur mighty high hill.

But de vay naix day Mistah B'ar he daid;
W'en dee tell Doc' Hyar, he des scratch he haid:

"Ef pahsons git well ur pahsons git wu's,
Money got ter come een de Ol' Hyar's pu's;
Not wut folkses does, but fur wut dee know
Does de folkses git paid"—an' Hyar larfed low,
                              Dis sma't Ol' Hyar,
                              Whar lib up dar
Een ur mighty fine house on ur mighty high hill!

WHEN OL' SIS' JUDY PRAY

When ol' Sis' Judy pray,
De teahs come stealin' down my cheek,
De voice ur God widin me speak';
I see myse'f so po' an' weak,
Down on my knees de cross I seek,
When ol' Sis' Judy pray.

When ol' Sis' Judy pray,
De thun'ers ur Mount Sin-a-i
Comes rushin' down f'um up on high—
De Debbil tu'n his back an' fly
While sinnahs loud fur pa'don cry,
When ol' Sis' Judy pray.

When ol' Sis' Judy pray,
Ha'd sinnahs trimble in dey seat
Ter hyuh huh voice in sorro' 'peat:
(While all de chu'ch des sob an' weep)
"O Shepa'd, dese, dy po' los' sheep!"
When ol' Sis' Judy pray.

When ol' Sis' Judy pray,
De whole house hit des rock an' moan
Ter see huh teahs an' hyuh huh groan;
Dar's somepin' in Sis' Judy's tone
Dat melt all ha'ts dough med ur stone
When ol' Sis' Judy pray.

When ol' Sis' Judy pray,
Salvation's light comes pourin' down—
Hit fill de chu'ch an' all de town—
Why, angels' robes go rustlin' 'roun',
An' hebben on de Yurf am foun',
When ol' Sis Judy pray.

When ol' Sis' Judy pray,
My soul go sweepin' up on wings,
An' loud de chu'ch wid "Glory!" rings,
An' wide de gates ur Jahsper swings
Twel you hyuh ha'ps wid golding strings,
When ol' Sis' Judy pray. . . .

COMPENSATION

O, rich young lord, thou ridest by
With looks of high disdain;
It chafes me not thy title high,
Thy blood of oldest strain.
The lady riding at thy side
Is but in name thy promised bride,
    Ride on, young lord, ride on!

Her father wills and she obeys,
The custom of her class;

'Tis Land not Love the trothing sways—
For Land he sells his lass.
Her fair white hand, young lord, is thine,
Her *soul*, proud fool, her *soul* is mine,
        Ride on, young lord, ride on!

No title high my father bore;
The tenant of thy farm,
He left me what I value more:
Clean heart, clear brain, strong arm
And love for bird and beast and bee
And song of lark and hymn of sea,
        Ride on, young lord, ride on!

The boundless sky to me belongs,
The paltry acres thine;
The painted beauty sings thy songs,
The laverock lilts me mine;
The hot-housed orchid blooms for thee,
The gorse and heather bloom for me,
        Ride on, young lord, ride on!

JAMES DAVID CORROTHERS

J AMES DAVID CORROTHERS *was born in Cass County, Michigan, in 1869. His mother died at his birth and his father gave him very little care or attention. During his youth he gained a livelihood through many kinds of occupation. He worked in the saw mills and lumber camps of his native state, was a sailor on the lakes, a coachman, a janitor, and for a time a bootblack in a barber shop. Through friends, two of them Henry D. Lloyd and Frances E. Willard, he was encouraged to get an education. As a young man he entered the ministry, and continued in that profession throughout his life.*

Corrothers wrote a number of poems that were first published in the Century *Magazine. These poems attracted wide attention. National sentiment of a generation ago made his "At the Closed Gates of Justice" a much-quoted poem. Considered in its time and within the limits of its mood, it is a moving poem. And, too, it is a poem that no Negro poet of today would think of writing. In spirit he shows kinship with some of the pre-Dunbar poets; but, of course, is beyond comparison with them in scholarship and skill. His dialect poetry is modeled closely after Dunbar's.*

He is the author of two volumes of poetry, Selected Poems *(1907) and* The Dream and the Song *(1914). He also published* The Black Cat Club, *a series of sketches originally contributed as special articles to several of the Chicago daily newspapers, and* In Spite of Handicap *(1916), an autobiography.*

AT THE CLOSED GATE OF JUSTICE

To be a Negro in a day like this
   Demands forgiveness. Bruised with blow on blow,
Betrayed, like him whose woe dimmed eyes gave bliss,
   Still must one succor those who brought one low,
To be a Negro in a day like this.

To be a Negro in a day like this
   Demands rare patience—patience that can wait
In utter darkness. 'Tis the path to miss,
   And knock, unheeded, at an iron gate,
To be a Negro in a day like this.

To be a Negro in a day like this
   Demands strange loyalty. We serve a flag
Which is to us white freedom's emphasis.
   Ah! one must love when Truth and Justice lag,
To be a Negro in a day like this.

To be a Negro in a day like this—
   Alas! Lord God, what evil have we done?
Still shines the gate, all gold and amethyst,
   But I pass by, the glorious goal unwon,
"Merely a Negro"—in a day like this!

PAUL LAURENCE DUNBAR

He came, a youth, singing in the dawn
   Of a new freedom, glowing o'er his lyre,
   Refining, as with great Apollo's fire,
   His people's gift of song. And thereupon,
This Negro singer, come to Helicon,

Constrained the masters, listening to admire,
And roused a race to wonder and aspire,
Gazing which way their honest voice was gone,
With ebon face uplit of glory's crest.
Men marveled at the singer, strong and sweet,
Who brought the cabin's mirth, the tuneful night,
But faced the morning, beautiful with light,
To die while shadows yet fell toward the west,
And leave his laurels at his people's feet.

Dunbar, no poet wears your laurels now;
None rises, singing, from your race like you.
Dark melodist, immortal, though the dew
Fell early on the bays upon your brow,
And tinged with pathos every halcyon vow
And brave endeavor. Silence o'er you threw
Flowerets of love. Or, if an envious few
Of your own people brought no garlands, how
Could malice smite him whom the gods had crowned?
If, like the meadow-lark, your flight was low,
Your flooded lyrics half the hilltops drowned;
A wide world heard you, and it loved you so,
It stilled its heart to list the strains you sang,
And o'er your happy songs its plaudits rang.

THE NEGRO SINGER

O'er all my song the image of a face
Lieth, like shadow on the wild sweet flowers.
The dream, the ecstasy that prompts my powers;
The golden lyre's delights bring little grace
To bless the singer of a lowly race.

Long hath this mocked me: aye in marvelous hours,
When Hera's gardens gleamed, or Cynthia's bowers,
Or Hope's red pylons, in their far, hushed place!
But I shall dig me deeper to the gold;
Fetch water, dripping, over desert miles,
From clear Nyanzas and mysterious Niles
Of love; and sing, nor one kind act withhold.
So shall men know me, and remember long,
Nor my dark face dishonor any song.

THE ROAD TO THE BOW

Ever and ever anon,
After the black storm, the eternal, beauteous bow!
Brother, to rosy-painted mists that arch beyond,
Blithely I go.

My brows men laureled and my lyre
Twined with immortal ivy for one little rippling song;
My "House of Golden Leaves" they praised and "passionate
fire"—
But, Friend, the way is long!

Onward and onward, up! away!
Though Fear flaunt all his banners in my face,
And my feet stumble, lo! the Orphean Day!
Forward by God's grace!

These signs are still before me: "Fear,"
"Danger," "Unprecedented," and I hear black "No"
Still thundering, and "Churl." Good Friend, I rest me
here—
Then to the glittering bow!

Loometh and cometh Hate in wrath,
  Mailed Wrong, swart Servitude and Shame with bitter
    rue,
Nathless a Negro poet's feet must tread the path
  The winged god knew.

Thus, my true Brother, dream-led, I
  Forfend the anathema, following the span.
I hold my head as proudly high
  As any man.

IN THE MATTER OF TWO MEN

One does such work as one will not,
  And well each knows the right;
Though the white storm howls, or the sun is hot,
  The black must serve the white.
And it's, oh, for the white man's softening flesh,
  While the black man's muscles grow!
Well I know which grows the mightier,
  I know; full well I know.

The white man seeks the soft, fat place,
  And he moves and he works by rule.
Ingenious grows the humbler race
  In Oppression's prodding school.
And it's, oh, for a white man gone to seed,
  While the Negro struggles so!
And I know which race develops most,
  I know; yes, well I know.

The white man rides in a palace car,
  And the Negro rides "Jim Crow."
To damn the other with bolt and bar,
  One creepeth so low; so low!
And it's, oh, for a master's nose in the mire,
  While the humbled hearts o'erflow!
Well I know whose soul grows big at this,
  And whose grows small; *I know!*

The white man leases out his land,
  And the Negro tills the same.
One works; one loafs and takes command;
  But I know who wins the game!
And it's, oh, for the white man's shrinking soil,
  As the black's rich acres grow!
Well I know how the signs point out at last,
  I know; ah, well I know!

The white man votes for his color's sake,
  While the black, for his is barred;
(Though "ignorance" is the charge they make),
  But the black man studies hard.
And it's, oh, for the white man's sad neglect,
  For the power of his light let go!
So, I know which man must win at last,
  I know! Ah, Friend, I know!

AN INDIGNATION DINNER

Dey was hard times jes fo' Christmas round our neighbor-
    hood one year;
So we held a secret meetin', whah de white folks couldn't
    hear,

To 'scuss de situation, an' to see what could be done
Towa'd a fust-class Christmas dinneh an' a little Christmas
fun.

Rufus Green, who called de meetin', ris an' said: "In dis
here town,
An' throughout de land, de white folks is a'tryin' to keep
us down."
S' 'e: "Dey bought us, sold us, beat us; now dey 'buse us
'ca'se we's free;
But when dey tetch my stomach, dey's done gone too fur
foh me!

"Is I right?" "You sho is, Rufus!" roared a dozen hungry
throats.
"Ef you'd keep a mule a-wo'kin', don't you tamper wid his
oats.
Dat's sense," continued Rufus. "But dese white folks nowa-
days
Has done got so close and stingy you can't live on what dey
pays.

"Here 'tis Christmas-time, an', folkses, I's indignant 'nough
to choke.
Whah's our Christmas dinneh comin' when we's 'mos' com-
pletely broke?
I can't hahdly 'fo'd a toothpick an' a glass o' water. Mad?
Say, I'm desp'ret! Dey jes better treat me nice, dese white
folks had!"

Well, dey 'bused de white folks scan'lous, till old Pappy
Simmons ris,
Leanin' on his cane to s'pote him, on account his rheu-
matis',

An' s' 'e: "Chilun, whut's dat wintry wind a-sighin' th'ough
    de street
'Bout yo' wasted summeh wages? But, no matter, we mus'
    eat.

"Now, I seed a beau'ful tuhkey on a certain gemmun's
    fahm.
He's a-growin' fat an' sassy, an' a-struttin' to a chahm.
Chickens, sheeps, hogs, sweet pertaters—all de craps is fine
    dis year;
All we needs is a committee foh to tote de goodies here."

Well, we lit right in an' voted dat it was a gran' idee,
An' de dinneh we had Christmas was worth trabblin' miles
    to see;
An' we eat a full an' plenty, big an' little, great an' small,
Not beca'se we was dishonest, but indignant, sah. Dat's all.

DREAM AND THE SONG

So oft our hearts, belovèd lute,
In blossomy haunts of song are mute;
So long we pore, 'mid murmurings dull,
O'er loveliness unutterable.
So vain is all our passion strong!
The dream is lovelier than the song.

The rose thought, touched by words, doth turn
Wan ashes. Still, from memory's urn,
The lingering blossoms tenderly
Refute our wilding minstrelsy.
Alas! we work but beauty's wrong!
The dream is lovelier than the song.

Yearned Shelley o'er the golden flame?
Left Keats for beauty's lure, a name
But "writ in water"? Woe is me!
To grieve o'er flowerful faëry.
My Phasian doves are flown so long—
The dream is lovelier than the song!

Ah, though we build a bower of dawn,
The golden-wingèd bird is gone,
And morn may gild, through shimmering leaves,
Only the swallow-twittering eaves.
What art may house or gold prolong
A dream far lovelier than a song?

The lilting witchery, the unrest
Of wingèd dreams, is in our breast;
But ever dear Fulfillment's eyes
Gaze otherward. The long-sought prize,
My lute, must to the gods belong.
The dream is lovelier than the song.

DANIEL WEBSTER DAVIS

D ANIEL WEBSTER DAVIS *was born in North Carolina in 1862. His parents moved to Richmond, Virginia, immediately after the Civil War, and the boy attended school in that city. He finished high school in 1878 with a high record for scholarship, and in 1880 began to teach in the Richmond colored public schools; later, in 1885, he went into the ministry. In 1897 he published his collected verse in a volume entitled 'Weh Down Souf. His poetry achieved wide popularity among the less literate of his own race. As a preacher-orator—typical of the period—he was noted, and used to read his verses with comical unctuousness before convulsed audiences. His work, placed beside Dunbar's, is distinguished chiefly by its crudity. It also furnishes splendid examples of the artificial sentiment and false minstrel tradition that make so much Negro dialect poetry of his day unreadable now. He was also the author of the Exposition Ode written for the opening of the Negro Building at the Atlanta Cotton Exposition, 1895; a poem which expresses a certain degree of pride and aspiration but, in the main, carries the "plantation tradition" over into straight English.*

'WEH DOWN SOUF

O, de birds ar' sweetly singin',
      'Weh down Souf,
An' de banjer is a-ringin',
      'Weh down Souf;

An' my heart it is a-sighin',
Whil' de moments am a-flyin',
Fur my hom' I am a-cryin',
    'Weh down Souf.

Dar de pickaninnies 's playin',
    'Weh down Souf,
An' fur dem I am a-prayin',
    'Weh down Souf;
An' when I gits sum munny,
Yo' kin bet I'm goin', my hunny,
Fur de lan' dat am so sunny,
    'Weh down Souf.

Whil' de win' up here's a-blowin',
    'Weh down Souf
De corn is sweetly growin',
    'Weh down Souf.
Dey tells me here ub freedum,
But I ain't a-gwine to heed um,
But I'se gwine fur to lebe um,
    Fur 'weh down Souf.

I bin up here a'-wuckin',
    From 'weh down Souf,
An' I ain't a bin a-shurkin'—
    I'm frum 'weh down Souf;
But I'm gittin' mighty werry,
An' de days a-gittin' drerry,
An' I'm hongry, O, so berry,
    Fur my hom' down Souf.

O, de moon dar shines de brighter,
        'Weh down Souf,
An' I know my heart is lighter,
        'Weh down Souf;
An' de berry thought brings pledjur,
I'll be happy dar 'dout medjur,
Fur dar I hab my tredjur,
        'Weh down Souf.

HOG MEAT

Deze eatin' folks may tell me ub de gloriz ub spring lam',
An' de toofsumnis ub tuckey et wid cel'ry an' wid jam;
Ub beef-st'ak fried wid unyuns, an' sezoned up so fine—
But yo' jes' kin gimme hog-meat, an' I'm happy all de
    time.

When de fros' is on de pun'kin an' de sno'-flakes in de a'r,
I den begin rejoicin'—hog-killin' time is near;
An' de vizhuns ub de fucher den fill my nightly dreams,
Fur de time is fas' a-comin' fur de 'lishus pork an' beans.

We folks dat's frum de kuntry may be behin' de sun—
We don't like city eatin's, wid beefsteaks dat ain' done—
Dough mutton chops is splendid, an' dem veal cutlits fine,
To me 'tain't like a sphar-rib, or gret big chunk ub chine.

Jes' talk to me 'bout hog-meat, ef yo' want to see me pleased,
Fur biled wid beans tiz gor'jus, or made in hog-head cheese;
An' I could jes' be happy, 'dout money, cloze or house,
Wid plenty yurz an' pig feet made in ol'-fashun "souse."

I 'fess I'm only human, I hab my joys an' cares—
Sum days de clouds hang hebby, sum days de skies ar' fair;
But I forgib my in'miz, my heart is free frum hate,
When my bread is filled wid cracklins an' dar's chidlins on
    my plate.

Dough 'possum meat is glo'yus wid 'taters in de pan,
But put 'longside pork sassage it takes a backward stan';
Ub all yer fancy eatin's, jes' gib to me fur mine
Sum souse or pork or chidlins, sum sphar-rib, or de chine.

WILLIAM H. A. MOORE

WILLIAM H. A. MOORE *was born in New York City and received his education in the public schools and at City College. He has had a long career in newspaper work, and is the author of* Dusk Songs, *a volume of poems. Moore's poems are cast in a conventional mold and cannot be said to possess unusual distinction; they are in a melancholy mood and of a very even tenor, with scarcely any rise or fall; yet they do at times attain a quiet beauty.*

DUSK SONG

The garden is very quiet tonight,
The dusk has gone with the Evening Star,
And out on the bay a lone ship light
Makes a silver pathway over the bar,
Where the sea sings low.

I follow the light with an earnest eye,
Creeping along to the thick far-away,
Until it fell in the depths of the deep, dark sky
With the haunting dream of the dusk of day
And its lovely glow.

Long nights, long nights and the whisperings of new ones,
Flame the line of the pathway down to the sea
With the halo of new dreams and the hallow of old ones,
And they bring magic light to my love reverie
And a lover's regret.

Tender sorrow for loss of a soft murmured word,
Tender measure of doubt in a faint, aching heart,
Tender listening for wind-songs in the tree heights heard
When you and I were of the dusks a part,
Are with me yet.

I pray for faith to the noble spirit of Space,
I sound the cosmic depths for the measure of glory
Which will bring to this earth the imperishable race
Of whom Beauty dreamed in the soul-toned story
The Prophets told.

Silence and love and deep wonder of stars
Dust-silver the heavens from west to east,
From south to north, and in a maze of bars
Invisible I wander far from the feast,
As night grows old.

Half blind is my vision I know to the truth,
My ears are half deaf to the voice of the tear
That touches the silences as Autumn's ruth
Steals through the dusks of each returning year,
A goodly friend.

The Autumn, then Winter and wintertime's grief!
But the weight of the snow is the glistening gift
Which loving brings to the rose and its leaf,
For the days of the roses glow in the drift
And never end.

. . . .

The moon has come. Wan and pallid is she.
The spell of half memories, the touch of half tears,
And the wounds of worn passions she brings to me
With all the tremor of the far-off years
And their mad wrong.

Yet the garden is very quiet tonight,
The dusk has long gone with the Evening Star,
And out on the bay the moon's wan light
Lays a silver pathway beyond the bar,
Dear heart, pale and long.

IT WAS NOT FATE

It was not fate which overtook me,
Rather a wayward, willful wind
That blew hot for a while
And then, as the even shadows came, blew cold.
What pity it is that a man grown old in life's dreaming
Should stop, e'en for a moment, to look into a woman's eyes.
And I forgot!
Forgot that one's heart must be steeled against the east wind.
Life and death alike come out of the East:
Life as tender as young grass,
Death as dreadful as the sight of clotted blood.
I shall go back into the darkness,
Not to dream but to seek the light again.
I shall go by paths, mayhap,
On roads that wind around the foothills
Where the plains are bare and wild
And the passers-by come few and far between.
I want the night to be long, the moon blind,

The hills thick with moving memories,
And my heart beating a breathless requiem
For all the dead days I have lived.
When the Dawn comes—Dawn, deathless, dreaming—
I shall will that my soul must be cleansed of hate,
I shall pray for strength to hold children close to my heart,
I shall desire to build houses where the poor will know shelter, comfort, beauty.
And then may I look into a woman's eyes
And find holiness, love and the peace which passeth understanding.

W. E. BURGHARDT DU BOIS

W. E. BURGHARDT DU BOIS *was born at Great Barrington, Mass., 1868. He was educated in the public schools of his native town and at Fisk University, Harvard University, and the University of Berlin. He was for a while a teacher at Wilberforce University and for a number of years professor of economics and history at Atlanta University. As a writer he is known almost entirely by his prose; and in that field he ranks high in American literature. He has written practically no formal poetry, but often his prose rises to where it is hardly distinguishable from poetry. In "A Litany of Atlanta" we have an example of language transcending its prosaic form. The poem, and such it truly is, was occasioned by the Atlanta race riot in 1906. It is a cry of grief and supplication, but it is steeped in irony and sarcasm. These two qualities are found double-distilled in such lines as:*

> Surely Thou too art not white, O Lord,
> a pale, bloodless, heartless thing?

But this same ironic and sarcastic note is developed and modulated into a chord of great beauty, marred only by the too closely recurring sibilants:

> Thou art still the God of our black fathers, and in
> Thy soul's soul sit some soft darkenings of the
> evening, some shadowings of the velvet night.

The prose works of Du Bois include The Souls of Black Folk (*1903*), The Suppression of the Slave Trade (*1896*),

89

The Negro (*1915*), John Brown, *a biography* (*1909*), Darkwater (*1921*), The Gift of Black Folk (*1924*), *and* The Quest of The Silver Fleece (*1911*) *and* The Dark Princess (*1928*), *two novels. He is the editor of* The Crisis. *In 1920 he was awarded the Spingarn Medal.*

A LITANY OF ATLANTA

Done at Atlanta, in the Day of Death, 1906.

O Silent God, Thou whose voice afar in mist and mystery hath left our ears an-hungered in these fearful days—
Hear us, good Lord!

Listen to us, Thy children: our faces dark with doubt are made a mockery in Thy sanctuary. With uplifted hands we front Thy heaven, O God, crying:
We beseech Thee to hear us, good Lord!

We are not better than our fellows, Lord, we are but weak and human men. When our devils do deviltry, curse Thou the doer and the deed: curse them as we curse them, do to them all and more than ever they have done to innocence and weakness, to womanhood and home.
Have mercy upon us, miserable sinners!

And yet whose is the deeper guilt? Who made these devils? Who nursed them in crime and fed them on injustice? Who ravished and debauched their mothers and their grandmothers? Who bought and sold their crime, and waxed fat and rich on public iniquity?
Thou knowest, good God!

Is this Thy justice, O Father, that guile be easier than innocence, and the innocent crucified for the guilt of the untouched guilty?

Justice, O judge of men!

Wherefore do we pray? Is not the God of the fathers dead? Have not seers seen in Heaven's halls Thine hearsed and lifeless form stark amidst the black and rolling smoke of sin, where all along bow bitter forms of endless dead?

Awake, Thou that sleepest!

Thou art not dead, but flown afar, up hills of endless light through blazing corridors of suns, where worlds do swing of good and gentle men, of women strong and free— far from the cozenage, black hypocrisy and chaste prostitution of this shameful speck of dust!

Turn again, O Lord, leave us not to perish in our sin!

From lust of body and lust of blood,
Great God, deliver us!

From lust of power and lust of gold,
Great God, deliver us!

From the leagued lying of despot and of brute,
Great God, deliver us!

A city lay in travail, God our Lord, and from her loins sprang twin Murder and Black Hate. Red was the midnight; clang, crack and cry of death and fury filled the air and trembled underneath the stars when church spires pointed silently to Thee. And all this was to sate the greed of greedy men who hide behind the veil of vengeance!

Bend us Thine ear, O Lord!

In the pale, still morning we looked upon the deed. We stopped our ears and held our leaping hands, but they—did they not wag their heads and leer and cry with bloody jaws: *Cease from Crime!* The word was mockery, for thus they train a hundred crimes while we do cure one.

Turn again our captivity, O Lord!

Behold this maimed and broken thing; dear God, it was an humble black man who toiled and sweat to save a bit from the pittance paid him. They told him: *Work and Rise.* He worked. Did this man sin? Nay, but some one told how some one said another did—one whom he had never seen nor known. Yet for that man's crime this man lieth maimed and murdered, his wife naked to shame, his children, to poverty and evil.

Hear us, O Heavenly Father!

Doth not this justice of hell stink in Thy nostrils, O God? How long shall the mounting flood of innocent blood roar in Thine ears and pound in our hearts for vengeance? Pile the pale frenzy of blood-crazed brutes who do such deeds high on Thine altar, Jehovah Jireh, and burn it in hell forever and forever!

Forgive us, good Lord; we know not what we say!

Bewildered we are, and passion-tost, mad with the madness of a mobbed and mocked and murdered people; straining at the armposts of Thy Throne, we raise our shackled hands and charge Thee, God, by the bones of our stolen fathers, by the tears of our dead mothers, by the very blood of Thy crucified Christ: *What meaneth this?* Tell us the Plan; give us the Sign!

Keep not Thou silence, O God!

Sit no longer blind, Lord God, deaf to our prayer and dumb to our dumb suffering. Surely Thou too art not white, O Lord, a pale, bloodless, heartless thing?
Ah! Christ of all the Pities!

Forgive the thought! Forgive these wild, blasphemous words. Thou art still the God of our black fathers, and in Thy soul's soul sit some soft darkenings of the evening, some shadowings of the velvet night.

But whisper—speak—call, great God, for Thy silence is white terror to our hearts! The way, O God, show us the way and point us the path.

Whither? North is greed and South is blood; within, the coward, and without, the liar. Whither? To death?
Amen! Welcome dark sleep!

Whither? To life? But not this life, dear God, not this. Let the cup pass from us, tempt us not beyond our strength, for there is that clamoring and clawing within, to whose voice we would not listen, yet shudder lest we must, and it is red, Ah! God! It is a red and awful shape.
Selah!

In yonder East trembles a star.
Vengeance is mine; I will repay, saith the Lord!

Thy will, O Lord, be done!
Kyrie Eleison!

Lord, we have done these pleading, wavering words.
We beseech Thee to hear us, good Lord!

We bow our heads and hearken soft to the sobbing of women and little children.

We beseech Thee to hear us, good Lord!

Our voices sink in silence and in night.

Hear us, good Lord!

In night, O God of a godless land!

Amen!

In silence, O Silent God.

Selah!

GEORGE MARION McCLELLAN

G EORGE MARION MC CLELLAN *was born at Belfast,*
*Tenn., 1860. He was educated at Fisk University and
at the Hartford Theological Seminary. He is a gentle poet
of nature, of the seasons, of birds and flowers and woodland
scenes. His work is after the long-accepted patterns, but
possesses a distinct charm. His best poems are collected in*
The Path of Dreams *(1916). He is exceptional in that
writing when and where he did, this collection contains no
dialect poetry.*

THE HILLS OF SEWANEE

Sewanee Hills of dear delight,
    Prompting my dreams that used to be,
I know you are waiting me still tonight
    By the Unika Range of Tennessee.

The blinking stars in endless space,
    The broad moonlight and silvery gleams,
Tonight caress your wind-swept face,
    And fold you in a thousand dreams.

Your far outlines, less seen than felt,
    Which wind with hill propensities,
In moonlight dreams I see you melt
    Away in vague immensities.

And, far away, I still can feel
  Your mystery that ever speaks
Of vanished things, as shadows steal
  Across your breast and rugged peaks.

O dear blue hills, that lie apart,
  And wait so patiently down there,
Your peace takes hold upon my heart
  And makes its burden less to bear.

DOGWOOD BLOSSOMS

To dreamy languors and the violet mist
  Of early Spring, the deep sequestered vale
Gives first her paling-blue Miamimist,
  Where blithely pours the cuckoo's annual tale
Of Summer promises and tender green,
  Of a new life and beauty yet unseen.
The forest trees have yet a sighing mouth,
  Where dying winds of March their branches swing,
While upward from the dreamy, sunny South,
  A hand invisible leads on the Spring.

His rounds from bloom to bloom the bee begins
  With flying song, and cowslip wine he sups,
Where to the warm and passing southern winds,
  Azaleas gently swing their yellow cups.
Soon everywhere, with glory through and through,
  The fields will spread with every brilliant hue.
But high o'er all the early floral train,
  Where softness all the arching sky resumes,
The dogwood dancing to the winds' refrain,
  In stainless glory spreads its snowy blooms.

A BUTTERFLY IN CHURCH

What dost thou here, thou shining, sinless thing,
With many colored hues and shapely wing?
Why quit the open field and summer air
To flutter here? Thou hast no need of prayer.

'Tis meet that we, who this great structure built,
Should come to be redeemed and washed from guilt,
For we this gilded edifice within
Are come, with erring hearts and stains of sin.

But thou art free from guilt as God on high;
Go, seek the blooming waste and open sky,
And leave us here our secret woes to bear,
Confessionals and agonies of prayer.

THE FEET OF JUDAS

Christ washed the feet of Judas!
The dark and evil passions of his soul,
His secret plot, and sordidness complete,
His hate, his purposing, Christ knew the whole,
And still in love he stooped and washed his feet.

Christ washed the feet of Judas!
Yet all his lurking sin was bare to him,
His bargain with the priest, and more than this,
In Olivet, beneath the moonlight dim,
Aforehand knew and felt his treacherous kiss.

Christ washed the feet of Judas!
And so ineffable his love 'twas meet,
That pity fill his great forgiving heart,
And tenderly to wash the traitor's feet,
Who in his Lord had basely sold his part.

Christ washed the feet of Judas!
And thus a girded servant, self-abased,
Taught that no wrong this side the gate of heaven
Was ever too great to wholly be effaced,
And though unasked, in spirit be forgiven.

And so if we have ever felt the wrong
Of trampled rights, of caste, it matters not,
What e'er the soul has felt or suffered long,
Oh, heart! this one thing should not be forgot:
Christ washed the feet of Judas.

WILLIAM STANLEY BRAITHWAITE

WILLIAM STANLEY BRAITHWAITE *was born in Boston, 1878. He is mainly self-educated. As an Aframerican poet he is unique; he has written no poetry motivated or colored by race. This has not been a matter of intention on his part; it is simply that race has not impinged upon him as it has upon other Negro poets. In fact, his work is so detached from race that for many years he had been a figure in the American literary world before it was known generally that he is a man of color. Braithwaite's poetry is marked by delicate beauty, often tinged by mysticism or whimsy. Still, many of his poems reveal his philosophy of life. He is skilled in the subtleties of poetic effect, and when he wishes he is a superb lyrist.*

But Braithwaite's work as a poet is eclipsed by his work as an anthologist and critic. He was one of the pioneer forces in stimulating the "revival" of poetry in America, which began about 1912; and his name will always remain associated with the movement. He is the author of three volumes of poetry: Lyrics of Life (*1904*), The House of Falling Leaves (*1908*), *and* Sandy Star and Willie Gee (*1922*). *His anthologies are* The Book of Elizabethan Verse (*1906*), The Book of Georgian Verse (*1908*), The Book of Restoration Verse (*1909*), *and a series of yearly anthologies of magazine verse, begun in 1913. He is also the author of* The Lyric Year *and* The Story of the Great War. *He was for some years on the literary editorial staff of the* Boston Transcript. *He was awarded the Spingarn Medal in 1918.*

SANDY STAR AND WILLIE GEE

Sandy Star and Willie Gee,
Count 'em two, you make 'em three:
Pluck the man and boy apart
And you'll see into my heart.

SANDY STAR

I

Sculptured Worship

The zones of warmth around his heart,
  No alien airs had crossed;
But he awoke one morn to feel
  The magic numbness of autumnal frost.

His thoughts were a loose skein of threads,
  And tangled emotions, vague and dim;
And sacrificing what he loved
  He lost the dearest part of him.

In sculptured worship now he lives,
  His one desire a prisoned ache;
If he can never melt again
  His very heart will break.

II

Laughing It Out

He had a whim and laughed it out
  Upon the exit of a chance;
He floundered in a sea of doubt—
  If life was real—or just romance.

Sometimes upon his brow would come
  A little pucker of defiance;
He totaled in a word the sum
  Of all man made of facts and science.

And then a hearty laugh would break,
  A reassuring shrug of shoulder;
And we would from his fancy take
  A faith in death which made life bolder.

III

Exit

No, his exit by the gate
  Will not leave the wind ajar;
He will go when it is late
  With a misty star.

One will call, he cannot see;
  One will call, he will not hear;
He will take no company
  Nor a hope or fear.

We shall smile who loved him so—
    They who gave him hate will weep;
But for us the winds will blow
    Pulsing through his sleep.

IV

The Way

He could not tell the way he came,
    Because his chart was lost:
Yet all his way was paved with flame
    From the bourne he crossed.

He did not know the way to go,
    Because he had no map:
He followed where the winds blow—
    And the April sap.

He never knew upon his brow
    The secret that he bore,—
And laughs away the mystery now
    The dark's at his door.

V

Onus Probandi

No more from out the sunset,
    No more across the foam,
No more across the windy hills
    Will Sandy Star come home.

He went away to search it
  With a curse upon his tongue;
And in his hand the staff of life,
  Made music as it swung.

I wonder if he found it,
  And knows the mystery now—
Our Sandy Star who went away,
  With the secret on his brow.

DEL CASCAR

Del Cascar, Del Cascar,
Stood upon a flaming star,
Stood, and let his feet hang down
Till in China the toes turned brown.

And he reached his fingers over
The rim of the sea, like sails from Dover,
And caught a Mandarin at prayer,
And tickled his nose in Orion's hair.

The sun went down through crimson bars,
And left his blind face battered with stars—
But the brown toes in China kept
Hot the tears Del Cascar wept.

TURN ME TO MY YELLOW LEAVES

Turn me to my yellow leaves,
I am better satisfied;
There is something in me grieves—
That was never born, and died.

Let me be a scarlet flame
On a windy autumn morn,
I who never had a name,
Nor from breathing image born.
From the margin let me fall
Where the farthest stars sink down,
And the void consumes me,—all
In nothingness to drown.
Let me dream my dream entire,
Withered as an autumn leaf—
Let me have my vain desire,
Vain—as it is brief.

IRONIC: LL.D.

There are no hollows any more
Between the mountains; the prairie floor
Is like a curtain with the drape
Of the winds' invisible shape;
And nowhere seen and nowhere heard
The sea's quiet as a sleeping bird.

Now we're traveling, what holds back
Arrival, in the very track
Where the urge put forth; so we stay
And move a thousand miles a day
Time's a Fancy ringing bells
Whose meaning, charlatan history, tells!

SCINTILLA

I kissed a kiss in youth
 Upon a dead man's brow;
And that was long ago—
 And I'm a grown man now.

It's lain there in the dust,
 Thirty years and more—
My lips that set a light
 At a dead man's door.

SIC VITA

Heart free, hand free,
 Blue above, brown under,
All the world to me
 Is a place of wonder.
Sun shine, moon shine,
 Stars, and winds a-blowing,
All into this heart of mine
 Flowing, flowing, flowing!

Mind free, step free,
 Days to follow after,
Joys of life sold to me
 For the price of laughter.
Girl's love, man's love,
 Love of work and duty,
Just a will of God's to prove
 Beauty, beauty, beauty!

RHAPSODY

I am glad daylong for the gift of song,
For time and change and sorrow;
For the sunset wings and the world-end things
Which hang on the edge of tomorrow.
I am glad for my heart whose gates apart
Are the entrance-place of wonders,
Where dreams come in from the rush and din
Like sheep from the rains and thunders.

GEORGE REGINALD MARGETSON

GEORGE REGINALD MARGETSON *was born at St. Kitts, British West Indies, in 1877, and was educated in the Moravian school in his district. He came to the United States in 1897. He has found it necessary to work hard to support a large family, and his poems have been written in such moments as he could seize for that purpose. Among Aframerican poets he has a good claim to originality, even though his originality may contain echoes from Byron. Margetson attempted the use of satire, a literary weapon which—although it ought to be very effective in their hands—Negro poets have seemed scarcely aware of. He is the author of four volumes of poetry:* England in the West Indies (*1906*), Ethiopia's Flight (*1907*), Songs of Life (*1910*), The Fledgling Bard And The Poetry Society (*1916*).

The last-named volume is made up of a single poem that runs exactly one hundred pages. This poem is in many respects remarkable. It is written in a seven-line stanza, the first six lines containing five metrical feet, the closing line of the stanza being an Alexandrine, and the rhyme scheme a-b-a-b-b-c-c, with rhymes that are often surprising. It is interspersed with lyrical passages, some of which are of considerable length. The poem starts with the poet's quest of the Poetry Society, and as he proceeds he pauses to comment on many things: events current, social conditions, politics, the World War, the Negro problem, art, literature, religion. It reveals crudities, some of them, it seems, contrived by the author with his tongue in his cheek. It sags and wobbles in a good many places, and the shafts of satire do not always hit

the mark. But notwithstanding these and other faults, The
Fledgling Bard And The Poetry Society *remains, on the
whole, a most original volume. It is at many points amus-
ing, and at some points both witty and wise.*

STANZAS FROM

THE FLEDGLING BARD AND THE POETRY
SOCIETY

Part I

I'm out to find the new, the modern school,
Where Science trains the fledgling bard to fly,
Where critics teach the ignorant, the fool,
To write the stuff the editors would buy;
It matters not e'en though it be a lie—
Just so it aims to smash tradition's crown
And build up one instead decked with a new renown.

A thought is haunting me by night and day,
And in some safe archive I seek to lay it;
I have some startling thing I wish to say,
And they can put me wise just how to say it.
Without their aid, I, like the ass, must bray it,
Without due knowledge of its mood and tense,
And so 'tis sure to fail the bard to recompense.

Will some kind one direct me to that college
Where every budding genius now is headed,
The only source to gain poetic knowledge,
Where all the sacred truths lay deep imbedded,
Where nothing but the genuine goods are shredded—

The factory where they shape new feet and meters
That make poetic symbols sound like carpet beaters.

· · · · · · ·

I hope I'll be an eligible student,
E'en though I am no poet in a sense,
But just a hot-head youth with ways imprudent—
A rustic ranting rhymer like by chance
Who thinks that he can make the muses dance
By beating on some poet's borrowed lyre,
To win some fool's applause and please his own desire.

Perhaps they'll never know or e'en suspect
That I am not a true, a genuine poet;
If in the poet's colors I am decked
They may not ask me e'er to prove or show it.
I'll play the wise old cock, nor try to crow it,
But be content to gaze with open mind;
I'll never show the lead but eye things from behind.

· · · · · · ·

There goes a wench, a poor live human scrag,
Half crushed beneath the freight of seventy years,
With pail and scrub-brush, soapine and a rag,
To polish marble halls and dirty stairs.
I believe most times she cleans them with her tears,
Ah me, that's civilization at its height,
Democracy's full moon, obscured in darkest night.

· · · · · · ·

Our President is not a fighter,
   He is too proud to shoulder arms,
He is a scholar and a writer
   Who woos a wealthy widow's charms.

· · · · · · ·

The President,
A high-toned gent,
The darling son
Of Washington;
Has got the wit,
He makes a hit,
With campaign stuff
Of Yankee bluff.

. . . .

He wields his English and his grammar,
    His textbook and his rhetorics;
His words rain blows like a trip-hammer
    And cut much ice in politics.

He's getting wordier not wiser
    In trained and skilled diplomacy;
He holds the maniac-champ the Kaiser
    To strict accountability.

Come, Woody, quit your honeymooning;
    The Austrians have sunk a boat;
Cut out your wooing and your spooning,
    Get busy, write another note!

. . . . . .

The house of God is nigh forever closed,
While that of Baal is always open wide,
A poor religious zeal is here exposed,
Which thus reflects a lack of Christian pride.
From good to bad men daily turn aside,
As in a trice from heaven to hell they leap;
The devil works overtime while ministers hug sleep.

. . . .

We hail thee, land of liberty,
Star of our hope and destiny
Where long we've been and long must be
In freedom's fabled place.

We bless thee, land, in love's sweet name
Whereto as slaves our fathers came,
Where still we struggle lashed and lame,
As exiles torn from Grace.

The Scotchman tunes his pipe and drum,
Old Ireland's Harp is never dumb,
We make our rag-time banjo hum
To Uncle Sam's swift pace.

We follow where his footsteps lead,
We copy him in word and deed,
E'en though his low and vicious creed
Our morals should debase.

With him we hail the stripes and stars,
The stripes that stand for color bars,
The stars that burn and leave their scars
On our black bleeding race.

.   .   .   .   .

Some think this Negro question is a joke,
Exploited by their leaders for mere gain;
They have no time to fool with colored folk,
Who seem to show more energy than brain,
Who're always fighting, raising hell and cain
Among themselves; each wants a different leader,
They know no more their wants than donkeys know their
    breeder.

Some look to Booker Washington to lead them,
Some yell for Trotter, some for Kelly Miller,
Some want Du Bois with fat ideas to feed them,
Some want Jack Johnson, the big white hope killer.
Perhaps some want Carranza, some want Villa,
I guess they want social equality,
To marry and to mix in white society.

.   .   .   .   .   .

This is the white man's country,
And he must bear the sway;
The Negro is an outcast,
Who happens here to stray;
He bears upon his forehead
The badge of negligence,
By chance he drifted hither,
So he must live by chance.

The people rejoice to hear the nations say,
"The whites alone must bear the sway."

This is the native rampart
Of Nature's chosen sons,
While 'tis the haunted prison
Of her despised ones.
This is the fruitful Eden
Where fortune bids us dwell,
This is the white man's heaven,
But 'tis the Negro's hell.

The people laugh while all the nations yell,
"The white man's heaven is the black man's hell."

.   .   .   .

I have a problem all alone to solve,
A problem how to find the poetry club,
It makes my sky piece like a top revolve,
For fear that they might mark me for a snob.
They'll call me poetry monger and then dub
Me rustic rhymer, anything they choose,
Aye, anything at all, but heaven's immortal muse.

Great Byron, when he published his Childe book,
In which he sang of all his lovely dears,
Called forth hot condemnation and cold look,
From lesser mortals who were not his peers.
They chided him for telling his affairs,
Because they could not tell their own so well,
They plagued the poet lord and made his life a hell.

They called him lewd, vile drunkard, vicious wight,
And all because he dared to tell the truth,
Because he was no cursed hermaphrodite—
A full-fledged genius with the fire of youth.
They hounded him, they hammered him forsooth;
Because he blended human with divine,
They branded him "the bard of women and of wine."

Of course I soak the booze once in a while,
But I don't wake the town to sing and shout it;
I love the girls, they win me with a smile,
But no one knows, for I won't write about it.
And so the fools may never think to doubt it,
When I declare I am a moral man,
As gifted, yet as good as God did ever plan.

JAMES WELDON JOHNSON

I NTO *James Weldon Johnson's life has been crowded a*
great variety of experiences. He was born in Jacksonville,
Florida, in 1871, and educated in the schools of that city
and at Atlanta University. He served as principal of a gram-
mar school in Jacksonville for several years, developing it
into a high school within that time. He studied law and was
admitted to the Florida bar. In 1900 he wrote the national
Negro anthem, "Lift Every Voice and Sing," for which his
brother, J. Rosamond Johnson, composed the music. The
anthem is now sung generally by the colored people through-
out the country. In 1901 he and his brother moved to New
York and launched successfully into the work of writing
songs and musical plays. This work, however, did not use up
all of Johnson's energies; he found time to do graduate
study at Columbia University in literature and the drama.

From 1906 to 1913 he served as United States Consul,
first in Venezuela and then in Nicaragua, undergoing many
turbulent experiences. While in the consular service he wrote
The Autobiography of an Ex-Colored Man, *a novel, and*
contributed poems to The Century *and other magazines.*
He returned to New York in 1914. An able linguist, he was
called on to translate the libretto of the Spanish opera,
Goyescas, *produced in 1915 at the Metropolitan Opera*
House. *He next devoted his energies to the cause of the*
National Association for the Advancement of Colored
People, serving for fourteen years, first as field secretary and
then as secretary.

Diversified as his life has been, his writing has been just as versatile. Besides The Autobiography of an Ex-Colored Man (*1912*), *he is the author of* Fifty Years and Other Poems (*1917*), God's Trombones (*1927*), Black Manhattan (*1930*), *and* Saint Peter Relates an Incident of the Resurrection Day (*1930*), *and the editor of* The Book of American Negro Poetry (*1921*), The Book of American Negro Spirituals (*1925*), *and* The Second Book of American Negro Spirituals (*1926*), *the latter two in collaboration with J. Rosamond Johnson.*

As a novelist, James Weldon Johnson reveals in The Autobiography of an Ex-Colored Man *a breadth of knowledge concerning the Negro problem in all its ramifications, and a power both analytic and prophetic. In this book might be found the germinal idea of many later books dealing with the Negro. As a critic, he has been* par excellence *an introducer, an intermediary, an interpreter. Enthusiastically assured of his ground, he has sought to awaken a true evaluation of Negro contributions to American art and life. But only somewhat belatedly has the world come round to his way of thinking. The earlier* Book of Negro Poetry *was a pioneering venture in a fruitful field. In the first and second books of spirituals, James Weldon Johnson and J. Rosamond Johnson gave a definitive and much-needed edition of creations that America could little afford to lose.* Black Manhattan *tells engagingly the narrative of the Negro in New York.*

It is as a poet, however, that Johnson has achieved his finest effects. According to William Stanley Braithwaite, his first volume of poetry, Fifty Years and Other Poems, *"brought the first intellectual substance to the content of our poetry, and a craftsmanship . . . less spontaneous than Dunbar's, [but] more balanced and precise." To such poems as*

Fifty Years, *which Brander Matthews grouped with the noblest American commemorative poems, and* O Southland, The White Witch, *and* Brothers *he brought a virility and fire none the less powerful for being under firm control. In many of his lyrics there is the beauty of quiet sincerity.*

God's Trombones *startled critical acclaim. In this book were seven sermons and a prayer, couched in the polyrhythmic cadences of* The Creation. *Although in his earlier volume Johnson had included a dialect section, "Jingles and Croons," he nevertheless was convinced of the narrow limitations of traditional dialect. Wishing for these re-creations and interpretations of old Negro sermons the dignity, the sweep and splendor that are indisputably theirs, he turned to the model of Synge dealing with the Aran Islanders and sought to express "the racial symbol from within rather than from without." The enthusiastic reception of the poems established how right he was in his choice. Because of his great sympathy for subject matter which in lesser hands might have degenerated into grotesqueness Johnson has done more than the high task of "fixing something of the rapidly passing old-time Negro preacher." He has fashioned something of lasting beauty. Such poems as "Go Down, Death" and "Listen, Lord" must be placed among the noblest and most moving poems of American literature. The volume won the Harmon Gold Award for literature.*

An approach hitherto neglected by Negro poets is to be seen in Saint Peter Relates an Incident of the Resurrection Day. *For the greater part, in leisurely couplets, the poem comments ironically on American prejudices. Not at all blatant propaganda, the poem is incisive though restrained, and in the best sense witty. With its sly mockery it combines a deeply moving quality. In this most recent book are all the qualities of Johnson's best work: understanding, imagination, sincerity, and poise.*

He was awarded the Spingarn Medal in 1925.

STERLING A. BROWN

THE CREATION

(*A Negro Sermon from* GOD'S TROMBONES)

And God stepped out on space,
And he looked around and said:
I'm lonely—
I'll make me a world.

And far as the eye of God could see
Darkness covered everything,
Blacker than a hundred midnights
Down in a cypress swamp.

Then God smiled,
And the light broke,
And the darkness rolled up on one side,
And the light stood shining on the other,
And God said: That's good!

Then God reached out and took the light in His hands,
And God rolled the light around in His hands
Until He made the sun;
And He set that sun a-blazing in the heavens.
And the light that was left from making the sun
God gathered it up in a shining ball
And flung it against the darkness,

Spangling the night with the moon and stars.
Then down between
The darkness and the light
He hurled the world;
And God said: That's good!

Then God himself stepped down—
And the sun was on His right hand,
And the moon was on His left;
The stars were clustered about His head,
And the earth was under His feet.
And God walked, and where He trod
His footsteps hollowed the valleys out
And bulged the mountains up.

Then He stopped and looked and saw
That the earth was hot and barren.
So God stepped over to the edge of the world
And He spat out the seven seas—
He batted His eyes, and the lightnings flashed—
He clapped His hands, and the thunders rolled—
And the waters above the earth came down,
The cooling waters came down.

Then the green grass sprouted,
And the little red flowers blossomed,
The pine tree pointed his finger to the sky,
And the oak spread out his arms,
The lakes cuddled down in the hollows of the ground,
And the rivers ran down to the sea;
And God smiled again,
And the rainbow appeared,
And curled itself around His shoulder.

Then God raised His arm and He waved His hand
Over the sea and over the land,
And He said: Bring forth! Bring forth!
And quicker than God could drop His hand,
Fishes and fowls
And beasts and birds
Swam the rivers and the seas,
Roamed the forests and the woods,
And split the air with their wings.
And God said: That's good!

Then God walked around,
And God looked around
On all that He had made.
He looked at His sun,
And He looked at His moon,
And He looked at His little stars;
He looked on His world
With all its living things,
And God said: I'm lonely still.

Then God sat down—
On the side of a hill where He could think;
By a deep, wide river He sat down;
With His head in His hands,
God thought and thought,
Till He thought: I'll make me a man!

Up from the bed of the river
God scooped the clay;
And by the bank of the river
He kneeled Him down;

And there the great God Almighty
Who lit the sun and fixed it in the sky,
Who flung the stars to the most far corner of the night,
Who rounded the earth in the middle of His hand;
This Great God,
Like a mammy bending over her baby,
Kneeled down in the dust
Toiling over a lump of clay
Till He shaped it in His own image;

Then into it He blew the breath of life,
And man became a living soul.
Amen. Amen.

THE WHITE WITCH

O brothers mine, take care! Take care!
The great white witch rides out tonight.
Trust not your prowess nor your strength,
Your only safety lies in flight;
For in her glance there is a snare,
And in her smile there is a blight.

The great white witch you have not seen?
Then, younger brothers mine, forsooth,
Like nursery children you have looked
For ancient hag and snaggle-tooth;
But no, not so; the witch appears
In all the glowing charms of youth.

Her lips are like carnations, red,
Her face like new-born lilies, fair,

Her eyes like ocean waters, blue,
She moves with subtle grace and air,
And all about her head there floats
The golden glory of her hair.

But though she always thus appears
In form of youth and mood of mirth,
Unnumbered centuries are hers,
The infant planets saw her birth;
The child of throbbing Life is she,
Twin sister to the greedy earth.

And back behind those smiling lips,
And down within those laughing eyes,
And underneath the soft caress
Of hand and voice and purring sighs,
The shadow of the panther lurks,
The spirit of the vampire lies.

For I have seen the great white witch,
And she has led me to her lair,
And I have kissed her red, red lips
And cruel face so white and fair;
Around me she has twined her arms,
And bound me with her yellow hair.

I felt those red lips burn and sear
My body like a living coal;
Obeyed the power of those eyes
As the needle trembles to the pole;
And did not care although I felt
The strength go ebbing from my soul.

Oh! she has seen your strong young limbs,
And heard your laughter loud and gay,
And in your voices she has caught
The echo of a far-off day,
When man was closer to the earth;
And she has marked you for her prey.

She feels the old Antaean strength
In you, the great dynamic beat
Of primal passions, and she sees
In you the last besieged retreat
Of love relentless, lusty, fierce,
Love fain-ecstatic, cruel-sweet.

O brothers mine, take care! Take care!
The great white witch rides out tonight.
O younger brothers mine, beware!
Look not upon her beauty bright;
For in her glance there is a snare,
And in her smile there is a blight.

SENCE YOU WENT AWAY

Seems lak to me de stars don't shine so bright,
Seems lak to me de sun done loss his light,
Seems lak to me der's nothin' goin' right,
   Sence you went away.

Seems lak to me de sky ain't half so blue,
Seems lak to me dat ev'ything wants you,
Seems lak to me I don't know what to do,
   Sence you went away.

Seems lak to me dat ev'ything is wrong,
Seems lak to me de day's jes twice es long,
Seems lak to me de bird's forgot his song,
     Sencé you went away.

Seems lak to me I jes can't he'p but sigh,
Seems lak to me ma th'oat keeps gittin' dry,
Seems lak to me a tear stays in ma eye,
     Sence you went away.

O BLACK AND UNKNOWN BARDS

O black and unknown bards of long ago,
How came your lips to touch the sacred fire?
How, in your darkness, did you come to know
The power and beauty of the minstrel's lyre?
Who first from midst his bonds lifted his eyes?
Who first from out the still watch, lone and long,
Feeling the ancient faith of prophets rise
Within his dark-kept soul, burst into song?

Heart of what slave poured out such melody
As "Steal away to Jesus"? On its strains
His spirit must have nightly floated free,
Though still about his hands he felt his chains.
Who heard great "Jordan roll"? Whose starward eye
Saw chariot "swing low"? And who was he
That breathed that comforting, melodic sigh,
"Nobody knows de trouble I see"?

What merely living clod, what captive thing,
Could up toward God through all its darkness grope,
And find within its deadened heart to sing
These songs of sorrow, love and faith, and hope?

How did it catch that subtle undertone,
That note in music heard not with the ears?
How sound the elusive reed so seldom blown,
Which stirs the soul or melts the heart to tears.

Not that great German master in his dream
Of harmonies that thundered amongst the stars
At the creation, ever heard a theme
Nobler than "Go down, Moses." Mark its bars
How like a mighty trumpet-call they stir
The blood. Such are the notes that men have sung
Going to valorous deeds; such tones there were
That helped make history when Time was young.

There is a wide, wide wonder in it all,
That from degraded rest and servile toil
The fiery spirit of the seer should call
These simple children of the sun and soil.
O black slave singers, gone, forgot, unfamed,
You—you alone, of all the long, long line
Of those who've sung untaught, unknown, unnamed,
Have stretched out upward, seeking the divine.

You sang not deeds of heroes or of kings;
No chant of bloody war, no exulting pean
Of arms-won triumphs; but your humble strings
You touched in chord with music empyrean.
You sang far better than you knew; the songs
That for your listeners' hungry hearts sufficed
Still live,—but more than this to you belongs:
You sang a race from wood and stone to Christ.

MY CITY

When I come down to sleep death's endless night,
The threshold of the unknown dark to cross,
What to me then will be the keenest loss,
When this bright world blurs on my fading sight?
Will it be that no more I shall see the trees
Or smell the flowers or hear the singing birds
Or watch the flashing streams or patient herds?
No, I am sure it will be none of these.

But, ah! Manhattan's sights and sounds, her smells,
Her crowds, her throbbing force, the thrill that comes
From being of her a part, her subtle spells,
Her shining towers, her avenues, her slums—
O God! the stark, unutterable pity,
To be dead, and never again behold my city!

LISTEN, LORD

(*A Prayer from* GOD'S TROMBONES)

O Lord, we come this morning
Knee-bowed and body-bent
Before Thy throne of grace.
O Lord—this morning—
Bow our hearts beneath our knees,
And our knees in some lonesome valley.
We come this morning—
Like empty pitchers to a full fountain,
With no merits of our own.
O Lord—open up a window of heaven,

And lean out far over the battlements of glory,
And listen this morning.

Lord, have mercy on proud and dying sinners—
Sinners hanging over the mouth of hell,
Who seem to love their distance well.
Lord—ride by this morning—
Mount Your milk-white horse,
And ride-a this morning—
And in Your ride, ride by old hell,
Ride by the dingy gates of hell,
And stop poor sinners in their headlong plunge.

And now, O Lord, this man of God,
Who breaks the bread of life this morning—
Shadow him in the hollow of Thy hand,
And keep him out of the gunshot of the devil.
Take him, Lord—this morning—
Wash him with hyssop inside and out,
Hang him up and drain him dry of sin.
Pin his ear to the wisdom-post,
And make his words sledge hammers of truth—
Beating on the iron heart of sin.
Lord God, this morning—
Put his eye to the telescope of eternity,
And let him look upon the paper walls of time.
Lord, turpentine his imagination,
Put perpetual motion in his arms,
Fill him full of the dynamite of Thy power,
Anoint him all over with the oil of Thy salvation,
And set his tongue on fire.

And now, O Lord—
When I've done drunk my last cup of sorrow—
When I've been called everything but a child of God—
When I'm done traveling up the rough side of the moun-
    tain—
O—Mary's Baby—
When I start down the steep and slippery steps of death—
When this old world begins to rock beneath my feet—
Lower me to my dusty grave in peace
To wait for that great gittin'-up morning—Amen.

THE GLORY OF THE DAY WAS IN HER FACE

The glory of the day was in her face,
The beauty of the night was in her eyes.
And over all her loveliness, the grace
Of Morning blushing in the early skies.

And in her voice, the calling of the dove;
Like music of a sweet, melodious part.
And in her smile, the breaking light of love;
And all the gentle virtues in her heart.

And now the glorious day, the beauteous night,
The birds that signal to their mates at dawn,
To my dull ears, to my tear-blinded sight
Are one with all the dead, since she is gone.

BROTHERS

See! There he stands; not brave, but with an air
Of sullen stupor. Mark him well! Is he
Not more like brute than man? Look in his eye!

No light is there; none, save the glint that shines
In the now glaring, and now shifting orbs
Of some wild animal caught in the hunter's trap.

How came this beast in human shape and form?
Speak, man!—We call you man because you wear
His shape—How are you thus? Are you not from
That docile, child-like, tender-hearted race
Which we have known three centuries? Not from
That more than faithful race which through three wars
Fed our dear wives and nursed our helpless babes
Without a single breach of trust? Speak out!

I am, and am not.

Then who, why are you?

I am a thing not new, I am as old
As human nature. I am that which lurks,
Ready to spring whenever a bar is loosed;
The ancient trait which fights incessantly
Against restraint, balks at the upward climb;
The weight forever seeking to obey
The law of downward pull—and I am more:
The bitter fruit am I of planted seed;
The resultant, the inevitable end
Of evil forces and the powers of wrong.

Lessons in degradation, taught and learned,
The memories of cruel sights and deeds,
The pent-up bitterness, the unspent hate
Filtered through fifteen generations have

Sprung up and found in me sporadic life.
In me the muttered curse of dying men,
On me the stain of conquered women, and
Consuming me the fearful fires of lust,
Lit long ago, by other hands than mine.
In me the down-crushed spirit, the hurled-back prayers
Of wretches now long dead—their dire bequests—
In me the echo of the stifled cry
Of children for their bartered mothers' breasts.

I claim no race, no race claims me; I am
No more than human dregs; degenerate;
The monstrous offspring of the monster, Sin;
I am—just what I am. . . . The race that fed
Your wives and nursed your babes would do the same
Today, but I—
                    Enough, the brute must die!
Quick! Chain him to that oak! It will resist
The fire much longer than this slender pine.
Now bring the fuel! Pile it 'round him! Wait!
Pile not so fast or high! or we shall lose
The agony and terror in his face.

And now the torch! Good fuel that! the flames
Already leap head-high. Ha! hear that shriek!
And there's another! Wilder than the first.
Fetch water! Water! Pour a little on
The fire, lest it should burn too fast. Hold so!
Now let it slowly blaze again. See there!
He squirms! He groans! His eyes bulge wildly out,
Searching around in vain appeal for help!
Another shriek, the last! Watch how the flesh

Grows crisp and hangs till, turned to ash, it sifts
Down through the coils of chain that hold erect
The ghastly frame against the bark-scorched tree.

Stop! to each man no more than one man's share.
You take that bone, and you this tooth; the chain—
Let us divide its links; this skull, of course,
In fair division, to the leader comes.

And now his fiendish crime has been avenged;
Let us back to our wives and children.—Say,
What did he mean by those last muttered words,
"Brothers in spirit, brothers in deed are we"?

FIFTY YEARS

(1863-1913)

*On the Fiftieth Anniversary of the Signing of the
Emancipation Proclamation*

O brothers mine, today we stand
  Where half a century sweeps our ken,
Since God, through Lincoln's ready hand,
  Struck off our bonds and made us men.

Just fifty years—a winter's day—
  As runs the history of a race;
Yet, as we look back o'er the way,
  How distant seems our starting place!

Look farther back! Three centuries!
  To where a naked, shivering score,
Snatched from their haunts across the seas,
  Stood, wild-eyed, on Virginia's shore.

.   .   .   .   .

For never let the thought arise
 That we are here on sufferance bare;
Outcasts, asylumed 'neath these skies,
 And aliens without part or share.

This land is ours by right of birth,
 This land is ours by right of toil;
We helped to turn its virgin earth,
 Our sweat is in its fruitful soil.

Where once the tangled forest stood—
 Where flourished once rank weed and thorn—
Behold the path-traced, peaceful wood,
 The cotton white, the yellow corn.

To gain these fruits that have been earned,
 To hold these fields that have been won,
Our arms have strained, our backs have burned,
 Bent bare beneath a ruthless sun.

That Banner which is now the type
 Of victory on field and flood—
Remember, its first crimson stripe
 Was dyed by Attucks' willing blood.

And never yet has come the cry—
 When that fair flag has been assailed—
For men to do, for men to die,
 That we have faltered or have failed.

We've helped to bear it, rent and torn,
 Through many a hot-breath'd battle breeze
Held in our hands, it has been borne
 And planted far across the seas.

And never yet—O haughty Land,
　Let us, at least, for this be praised—
Has one black, treason-guided hand
　Ever against that flag been raised.

Then should we speak but servile words,
　Or shall we hang our heads in shame?
Stand back of new-come foreign hordes,
　And fear our heritage to claim?

No! stand erect and without fear,
　And for our foes let this suffice—
We've bought a rightful sonship here,
　And we have more than paid the price.

And yet, my brothers, well I know
　The tethered feet, the pinioned wings,
The spirit bowed beneath the blow,
　The heart grown faint from wounds and stings;

The staggering force of brutish might,
　That strikes and leaves us stunned and dazed;
The long, vain waiting through the night
　To hear some voice for justice raised.

Full well I know the hour when hope
　Sinks dead, and round us everywhere
Hangs stifling darkness, and we grope
　With hands uplifted in despair.

Courage! Look out, beyond, and see
　The far horizon's beckoning span!
Faith in your God-known destiny!
　We are a part of some great plan.

Because the tongues of Garrison
   And Phillips now are cold in death,
Think you their work can be undone?
   Or quenched the fires lit by their breath?

Think you that John Brown's spirit stops?
   That Lovejoy was but idly slain?
Or do you think those precious drops
   From Lincoln's heart were shed in vain?

That for which millions prayed and sighed,
   That for which tens of thousands fought,
For which so many freely died,
   God cannot let it come to naught.

JOHN WESLEY HOLLOWAY

J OHN WESLEY HOLLOWAY *was born in Merriweather
County, Ga., in 1865. His father, who learned to read
and write as a slave, became one of the first colored teachers
in Georgia, and saw to it that his son received the advan-
tages he had not. Holloway was educated at Clark Univer-
sity, Atlanta, Ga., and at Fisk University. He was for a
while a member of the Fisk Jubilee Singers. He has been a
teacher and is now a preacher. He is the author of* From the
Desert *(1919), a volume of poems. Holloway is a disciple
of Dunbar, although born before him—and a worthy one, as
may be judged from the musical lilt of "Miss Melerlee" and
"The Corn Song" and from the humor of "Calling the
Doctor." But some of his work, for example, "Black Mam-
mies," is spoiled by a too thick and obvious application of
artificial sentiment. The black mammy is material for better
poetry than this, and* From the Desert—*excluding the moral
and religious poems at the end—contains much poetry that
is better. Holloway's best work is that done in the dialect.*

MISS MELERLEE

Hello dar, Miss Melerlee!
Oh, you're pretty sight to see!
Sof' brown cheek, an' smilin' face,
An' willowy form chuck full o' grace—
De sweetes' gal Ah evah see,
An' Ah wush dat you would marry me!
Hello, Miss Melerlee!

Hello dar, Miss Melerlee!
You're de berry gal fo' me!
Pearly teef, an' shinin' hair,
An' silky arm so plump an' bare!
Ah lak yo' walk, Ah lak yo' clothes,
An' de way Ah love you—goodness knows!
    Hello, Miss Melerlee!

Hello dar, Miss Melerlee!
Dat's not yo' name, but it ought to be!
Ah nevah seed yo' face befo'
An' lakly won't again no mo';
But yo' sweet smile will follow me
Cla'r into eternity!
    Farewell, Miss Melerlee!

CALLING THE DOCTOR

Ah'm sick, doctor-man, Ah'm sick!
Gi' me some'n to he'p me quick,
    Don't—Ah'll die!

Tried mighty hard fo' to cure mahse'f;
Tried all dem t'ings on de pantry she'f;
Couldn't fin' not'in' a-tall would do,
    An' so Ah sent fo' you.

"Wha'd Ah take?" Well, le' me see:
Firs'—horhound drops an' catnip tea;
Den rock candy soaked in rum,
An' a good sized chunk o' camphor gum;
Next Ah tried was castor oil,

An' snakeroot tea brought to a boil;
Sassafras tea fo' to clean mah blood;
But none o' dem t'ings didn' do no good.
Den when home remedies seem to shirk,
Dem pantry bottles was put to work:

Blue-mass, laud-num, liver pills,
"Sixty-six, fo' fever an' chills,"
Ready Relief, an' A. B. C.,
An' half a bottle of X. Y. Z.
An' sev'al mo' Ah don't recall,
Dey nevah done no good at all.
Mah appetite begun to fail;
Ah fo'ced some clabber, about a pail,
Fo' mah ol' gran'ma always said
When yo' can't eat you're almost dead.

So Ah got scared an' sent for you.—
Now, doctor, see what you c'n do.
Ah'm sick, doctor-man. Gawd knows Ah'm sick!
Gi' me some'n to he'p me quick,
    Don't—Ah'll die!

THE CORN SONG

Jes' beyan a clump o' pines—
    Lis'n to 'im now!—
Hyah de jolly black boy,
    Singin', at his plow!
In de early mornin',
    Thoo de hazy air,
Loud an' clear, sweet an' strong
    Comes de music rare:

"O mah dovee, Who-ah!
Do you love me? Who-ah!
        Who-ah!"
An' as 'e tu'ns de cotton row,
Hyah 'im tell 'is ol' mule so;
    "Whoa! Har! Come 'ere!"

Don't yo' love a co'n song?
    How it stirs yo' blood!
Ever'body list'nin',
    In de neighborhood!
Standin' in yo' front do'
    In de misty mo'n,
Hyah de jolly black boy,
    Singin' in de co'n:

"O Miss Julie, Who-ah!
Love me truly, Who-ah!
        Who-ah!"
Hyah 'im scol' 'is mule so,
W'en 'e try to mek 'im go:
    "Gee! Whoa! Come 'ere!"

O you jolly black boy,
    Yod'lin' in de co'n,
Callin' to yo' dawlin',
    In de dewy mo'n,
Love 'er, boy, forevah,
    Yodel ever' day;
Only le' me lis'n,
    As yo' sing away:

"O mah dawlin'! Who-ah!
Hyah me callin'! Who-ah!
    Who-ah!"
Tu'n aroun' anothah row,
Holler to yo' mule so:
    "Whoa! Har! Come 'ere!"

BLACK MAMMIES

If Ah evah git to glory, an' Ah hope to mek it thoo,
Ah expec' to hyah a story, an' Ah hope you'll hyah it, too—
Hit'll kiver Maine to Texas, an' f'om Bosting to Miami—
Ov de highes' shaf' in glory, 'rected to de Negro Mammy.

You will see a lot o' Washington, an' Washington again;
An' good ol' Fathah Lincoln, tow'rin' 'bove de rest o' men;
But dar'll be a bunch o' women standin' hard up by de
    th'one,
An' dey'll all be black an' homely—'less de Virgin Mary's
    one.

Dey will be de talk of angels, dey will be de praise o' men,
An' de whi' folks would go crazy 'thout their Mammy folks
    again:
If it's r'ally true dat meekness makes you heir to all de
    eart',
Den our blessed, good ol' Mammies must 'a' been of noble
    birt'.

If de greates' is de servant, den Ah got to say o' dem,
Dey'll be standin' nex' to Jesus, sub to no one else but Him;
If de crown goes to de fait'ful, an' de palm de victors wear,
Dey'll be loaded down wid jewels more dan anybody dere.

She'd de hardes' road to trabel evah mortal had to pull;
But she knelt down in huh cabin till huh cup o' joy was full;
Dough ol' Satan tried to shake huh f'om huh knees wid
    scowl an' frown,
She jes' "clumb up Jacob's ladder," an' he nevah drug huh
    down.

She'd jes' croon above de babies, she'd jes' sing when t'ings
    went wrong,
An' no matter what de trouble, she would meet it wid a
    song;
She jes' prayed huh way to heaben, findin' comfort in de
    rod;
She jes' "stole away to Jesus," she jes' sung huh way to
    God!

She "kep' lookin' ovah Jurdan," kep' "a-trustin' in de
    word,"
Kep' a-lookin' fo "de char'et," kep' "a-waitin' fo' de
    Lawd,"
If she evah had a quavah of de shadder of a doubt,
It ain't nevah been discovahed, fo' she nevah sung it out;

But she trusted in de shadder, an' she trusted in de shine,
An' she longed fo' one possession: "dat heaben to be
    mine";
An' she prayed huh chil'en freedom, but she won huhse'f
    de bes',—
Peace on eart' amids' huh sorrows, an' up yonder heavenly
    res'!

FENTON JOHNSON

FENTON JOHNSON *was born in Chicago, May 7, 1888. He was educated in the public schools of that city and at Chicago University. He was one of the first Negro revolutionary poets. His earliest work was cast in conventional molds, and with the exception of "The Vision of Lazarus," a poem in blank verse of nearly three hundred lines which closes* A Little Dreaming, *this first volume was without marked distinction. In the same volume a number of the poems were in dialect, but in the war period he broke away from all traditions and ideas of Negro poetry, in both dialect and literary English. Moreover, he disregarded the accepted poetic forms, subjects, and language, adopted free verse, and in that formless form wrote poetry in which he voiced the disillusionment and · bitterness of feeling the Negro race was then experiencing. In some of this poetry he went further than protests against wrong or the moral challenges that the wronged can always fling against the wrongdoer; he sounded the note of fatalistic despair. It was his poetry written in this key that brought him recognition. The central idea of this poetry was startling. Doubtless its effect was in some degree due to the fact that it was an idea so foreign to any philosophy of life the Negro in America had ever preached or practiced. Fenton Johnson is the only Negro poet who has ever sounded this precise note. McKay came closer to it than any of the others in "If We Must Die." There he calls on his brothers to make a last fight, but even so, it is a fight he calls for. W. E. Burghardt Du Bois closes the caustic "A Litany of At-*

lanta" on a note of faith. After a poem like "Tired" there is nothing left to fight or even hope for. Yet, as can be plainly seen, these poems of despair possess tremendous power and do constitute Fenton Johnson's best work.

It is also a fact that Johnson belongs in that group of American poets who in the middle of the second decade of the century threw over the traditions of American poetry and became the makers of the "new" poetry. He was among those writers whose work appeared in Others *and in* Poetry, A Magazine of Verse. *He is the author of three volumes of poems:* A Little Dreaming (*1912*), Visions of Dusk (*1915*), *and* Songs of the Soil (*1916*). *He has devoted much time to journalism and has edited and published a literary magazine. As a poet, he has for ten years or more been almost silent.*

CHILDREN OF THE SUN

We are children of the sun,
    Rising sun!
Weaving Southern destiny,
Waiting for the mighty hour
When our Shiloh shall appear
With the flaming sword of right,
With the steel of brotherhood,
And emboss in crimson die
Liberty! Fraternity!

We are the star-dust folk,
    Striving folk!
Sorrow songs have lulled to rest;
Seething passions wrought through wrongs,

Led us where the moon rays dip
In the night of dull despair,
Showed us where the star gleams shine,
And the mystic symbols glow—
Liberty! Fraternity!

We have come through cloud and mist,
    Mighty men!
Dusk has kissed our sleep-born eyes,
Reared for us a mystic throne
In the splendor of the skies,
That shall always be for us,
Children of the Nazarene,
Children who shall ever sing
Liberty! Fraternity!

THE NEW DAY

From a vision red with war I awoke and saw the Prince of
    Peace hovering over No Man's Land.
Loud the whistles blew and the thunder of cannon was
    drowned by the happy shouting of the people.
From the Sinai that faces Armageddon I heard this chant
    from the throats of white-robed angels:

Blow your trumpets, little children!
From the East and from the West,
From the cities in the valley,
From God's dwelling on the mountain,
Blow your blast that Peace might know
She is Queen of God's great army.
With the crying blood of millions

We have written deep her name
In the Book of all the Ages;
With the lilies in the valley,
With the roses by the Mersey,
With the golden flower of Jersey
We have crowned her smooth young temples.
Where her footsteps cease to falter
Golden grain will greet the morning,
Where her chariot descends
Shall be broken down the altars
Of the gods of dark disturbance.
Nevermore shall men know suffering,
Nevermore shall women wailing
Shake to grief the God of Heaven.
From the East and from the West,
From the cities in the valley,
From God's dwelling on the mountain,
Little children, blow your trumpets!

From Ethiopia, groaning 'neath her heavy burdens, I heard
    the music of the old slave songs.
I heard the wail of warriors, dusk brown, who grimly
    fought the fight of others in the trenches of Mars.
I heard the plea of blood-stained men of dusk and the
    crimson in my veins leapt furiously.

Forget not, O my brothers, how we fought
In No Man's Land that peace might come again!
Forget not, O my brothers, how we gave
Red blood to save the freedom of the world!
We were not free, our tawny hands were tied;
But Belgium's plight and Serbia's woes we shared

Each rise of sun or setting of the moon.
So when the bugle blast had called us forth
We went not like the surly brute of yore
But, as the Spartan, proud to give the world
The freedom that we never knew nor shared.
These chains, O brothers mine, have weighed us down
As Samson in the temple of the gods;
Unloosen them and let us breathe the air
That makes the goldenrod the flower of Christ.
For we have been with thee in No Man's Land,
Through lake of fire and down to Hell itself;
And now we ask of thee our liberty,
Our freedom in the land of Stars and Stripes.

I am glad that the Prince of Peace is hovering over No
Man's Land.

TIRED

I am tired of work; I am tired of building up somebody
else's civilization.
Let us take a rest, M'Lissy Jane.
I will go down to the Last Chance Saloon, drink a gallon
or two of gin, shoot a game or two of dice and
sleep the rest of the night on one of Mike's barrels.
You will let the old shanty go to rot, the white people's
clothes turn to dust, and the Calvary Baptist Church
sink to the bottomless pit.
You will spend your days forgetting you married me and
your nights hunting the warm gin Mike serves the
ladies in the rear of the Last Chance Saloon.
Throw the children into the river; civilization has given

us too many. It is better to die than it is to grow up
and find out that you are colored.
Pluck the stars out of the heavens. The stars mark our
destiny. The stars marked my destiny.
I am tired of civilization.

THE BANJO PLAYER

There is music in me, the music of a peasant people.
I wander through the levee, picking my banjo and sing-
ing my songs of the cabin and the field. At the Last
Chance Saloon I am as welcome as the violets in
March; there is always food and drink for me there,
and the dimes of those who love honest music. Behind
the railroad tracks the little children clap their hands
and love me as they love Kris Kringle.
But I fear that I am a failure. Last night a woman called
me a troubadour. What is a troubadour?

THE SCARLET WOMAN

Once I was good like the Virgin Mary and the Minister's
wife.
My father worked for Mr. Pullman and white people's
tips; but he died two days after his insurance expired.
I had nothing, so I had to go to work.
All the stock I had was a white girl's education and a
face that enchanted the men of both races.
Starvation danced with me.
So when Big Lizzie, who kept a house for white men,
came to me with tales of fortune that I could reap
from the sale of my virtue I bowed my head to Vice.

Now I can drink more gin than any man for miles around.
Gin is better than all the water in Lethe.

LINES FROM
"THE VISION OF LAZARUS"

Another sate near him, whose harp of gold
Had sounded in the tents of Israel,
His robes were woven from the cloth of Tyre
And golden sandals bound his olive feet.
"I am that David, he whose psalms ye sing
When sounds the timbrel in the plains of Gad.
My garments, washed of every crimson stain,
I am a wearer of the laurel wreath,
My heart as free as when in Bethlehem
I caused the blades of grass to dance with glee;
My soul each eventide goes forth with God,
A humble servant to His mystic will;
And in the morning do I wander wide,
Along the cool of every haunt and vale.
There lies a still brook deep in Heaven's land
Where milk-white sheep may stray and quench their thirst,
And there I nurse my memories of one
I wooed when in the house of lordly Saul.
A virgin like the rose when glides the wind
From out the Southland in the old year's noon."

EDWARD SMYTH JONES

EDWARD SMYTH JONES *suddenly gained the attention of the public in 1910 when, spurred by an ambition to secure an education, he walked some hundreds of miles from his home in the South to Harvard University, reaching there toward the end of July. When he arrived in Cambridge he proceeded to camp the first night in Harvard Square and was arrested on a charge of vagrancy. His arrest gained him wide publicity. While in jail he wrote a poem, "Harvard Square," in which he recited how it was ambition to learn that had brought him to this sorry plight. This poem he exhibited in his defense to the judge in court, and it was published by the newspapers. Sentiment was created that led to his quick release. Sentiment, as a result of this incident, also enabled him to bring out in a volume,* The Sylvan Cabin *(1911), his collected verses. The title poem of the volume is an ambitious effort to celebrate the centenary of Abraham Lincoln's birth in an ode of two hundred lines. The tone of the poem is pitched high, but the construction of the verse is clumsy and the development of the theme is feeble. Jones's work is filled with blemishes, the result of the fault—not uncommon among aspiring poets—of adopting an outworn vocabulary. Yet often, as in the example here given, he achieves through simplicity and spontaneity a sweeping effect.*

A SONG OF THANKS

For the sun that shone at the dawn of spring,
For the flowers which bloom and the birds that sing,
For the verdant robe of the gray old earth,
For her coffers filled with their countless worth,
For the flocks which feed on a thousand hills,
For the rippling streams which turn the mills,
For the lowing herds in the lovely vale,
For the songs of gladness on the gale,—
From the Gulf and the Lakes to the Oceans' banks,—
Lord God of Hosts, we give Thee thanks!

For the farmer reaping his whitened fields,
For the bounty which the rich soil yields,
For the cooling dews and refreshing rains,
For the sun which ripens the golden grains,
For the bearded wheat and the fattened swine,
For the stallèd ox and the fruitful vine,
For the tubers large and cotton white,
For the kid and the lambkin frisk and blithe,
For the swan which floats near the river-banks,—
Lord God of Hosts, we give Thee thanks!

For the pumpkin sweet and the yellow yam,
For the corn and beans and the sugared ham,
For the plum and the peach and the apple red,
For the dear old press where the wine is tread,
For the cock which crows at the breaking dawn,
And the proud old "turk" at the farmer's barn,
For the fish which swim in the babbling brooks,
For the game which hide in the shady nooks,—

From the Gulf and the Lakes to the Oceans' banks—
Lord God of Hosts, we give Thee thanks!

For the sturdy oaks and the stately pines,
For the lead and the coal from the deep, dark mines,
For the silver ores of a thousand fold,
For the diamond bright and the yellow gold,
For the river boat and the flying train,
For the fleecy sail of the rolling main,
For the velvet sponge and the glossy pearl,
For the flag of peace which we now unfurl—
From the Gulf and the Lakes to the Oceans' banks—
Lord God of Hosts, we give Thee thanks!

For the lowly cot and the mansion fair,
For the peace and plenty together share,
For the Hand which guides us from above,
For Thy tender mercies, abiding love,
For the blessed home with its children gay,
For returnings of Thanksgiving Day,
For the bearing toils and the sharing cares,
We lift up our hearts in our songs and our prayers—
From the Gulf and the Lakes to the Oceans' banks—
Lord God of Hosts, we give Thee thanks!

BENJAMIN BRAWLEY

BENJAMIN BRAWLEY *has written a good deal of poetry, but is best known as a writer of prose. His published prose works include:* The Negro in Literature and Art *(1910);* A Short History of the American Negro *(1919);* A Short History of the English Drama *(1921);* A Social History of the American Negro *(1921);* A New Survey of English Literature *(1925).* The Negro in Literature and Art *has gone through several revised and enlarged editions. It was the first comprehensive book on the subject, and remains one of the most valuable. For two years Mr. Brawley was Professor of English at Howard University. Later he became Dean of Morehouse College, Atlanta, Ga. Since 1923 he has been Professor of English at Shaw University, Raleigh, N. C.*

MY HERO

(To Robert Gould Shaw)

Flushed with the hope of high desire,
   He buckled on his sword,
To dare the rampart ranged with fire,
   Or where the thunder roared;
Into the smoke and flame he went,
   For God's great cause to die—
A youth of heaven's element,
   The flower of chivalry.

This was the gallant faith, I trow,
   Of which the sages tell;

On such devotion long ago
  The benediction fell;
And never nobler martyr burned,
  Or braver hero died,
Than he who worldly honor spurned
  To serve the Crucified.

And Lancelot and Sir Bedivere
  May pass beyond the pale,
And wander over moor and mere
  To find the Holy Grail;
But ever yet the prize forsooth
  My hero holds in fee;
And he is Blameless Knight in truth,
  And Galahad to me.

CHAUCER

Gone are the sensuous stars, and manifold,
Clear sunbeams burst upon the front of night;
Ten thousand swords of azure and of gold
Give darkness to the dark and welcome light;
Across the night of ages strike the gleams,
And leading on the gilded host appears
An old man writing in a book of dreams,
And telling tales of lovers for the years;
Still Troilus hears a voice that whispers, Stay;
In Nature's garden what a mad rout sings!
Let's hear these motley pilgrims wile away
The tedious hours with stories of old things;
Or might some shining eagle claim
These lowly numbers for the House of Fame!

LESLIE PINCKNEY HILL

Leslie Pinckney Hill *was born at Lynchburg, Va.,*
1880, and was educated in the local public school, in
the high school of East Orange, N. J., and at Harvard
University. On graduation from Harvard he became teacher
of English and Education at Tuskegee Institute. He is now
the principal of the Cheyney Training School for Teachers
at Cheyney, Pa. He writes in a quiet, restrained, scholarly
tone, with a modicum of lyric ecstasy and with never any-
thing approaching abandon or a passionate break from deco-
rum. He is philosophical rather than lyrical. All the poems
in his first volume, The Wings of Oppression (*1921*), *are*
more or less in this vein. That this calmness of manner,
however, does not imply lack of intensity is demonstrated
by the serene power achieved in the sonnet, "So Quietly."
In 1928 he published Toussaint L'Ouverture—A Dramatic
History. *This is a play in five parts and thirty-five scenes,*
based on the life of the great Haitian liberator. It is written
in blank verse interspersed with brief prose and lyrical pas-
sages and is the most ambitious single poem attempted by
any present-day Negro poet. The theme is a stirring one and
the elevated tone of the poem is sustained, but the verse
lacks flexibility, the fault being largely due to the author's
falling into the practice of stressing unimportant mono-
syllabic words and placing an accent on unaccented last
syllables of trisyllabic words, in order to fill out five
iambics to the line—a practice that can hardly fail to pro-
duce the "wooden" effect in blank verse.

TUSKEGEE

Wherefore this busy labor without rest?
Is it an idle dream to which we cling,
Here where a thousand dusky toilers sing
Unto the world their hope? "Build we our best.
By hand and thought," they cry, "although unblessed."
So the great engines throb, and anvils ring,
And so the thought is wedded to the thing;
But what shall be the end, and what the test?
Dear God, we dare not answer, we can see
Not many steps ahead, but this we know—
If all our toilsome building is in vain,
Availing not to set our manhood free,
If envious hate roots out the seed we sow,
The South will wear eternally a stain.

CHRISTMAS AT MELROSE

Come home with me a little space
And browse about our ancient place,
Lay by your wonted troubles here
And have a turn of Christmas cheer.
These sober walls of weathered stone
Can tell a romance of their own,
And these wide rooms of devious line
Are kindly meant in their design.
Sometimes the north wind searches through,
But he shall not be rude to you.
We'll light a log of generous girth
For winter comfort, and the mirth

Of healthy children you shall see
About a sparkling Christmas tree.
Eleanor, leader of the fold,
Hermione with heart of gold,
Elaine with comprehending eyes,
And two more yet of coddling size,
Natalie pondering all that's said,
And Mary with the cherub head—
All these shall give you sweet content
And care-destroying merriment,
While one with true madonna grace
Moves round the glowing fire-place
Where father loves to muse aside
And grandma sits in silent pride.
And you may chafe the wasting oak,
Or freely pass the kindly joke
To mix with nuts and home-made cake
And apples set on coals to bake.
Or some fine carol we will sing
In honor of the Manger-King,
Or hear great Milton's organ verse
Or Plato's dialogue rehearse
What Socrates with his last breath
Sublimely said of life and death.
These dear delights we fain would share
With friend and kinsman everywhere,
And from our door see them depart
Each with a little lighter heart.

SUMMER MAGIC

So many cares to vex the day,
    So many fears to haunt the night,
My heart was all but weaned away
    From every lure of old delight.
Then summer came, announced by June,
    With beauty, miracle and mirth.
She hung aloft the rounding moon,
    She poured her sunshine on the earth
She drove the sap and broke the bud,
    She set the crimson rose afire.
She stirred again my sullen blood,
    And waked in me a new desire.
Before my cottage door she spread
    The softest carpet nature weaves,
And deftly arched above my head
    A canopy of shady leaves.
Her nights were dreams of jeweled skies,
    Her days were bowers rife with song,
And many a scheme did she devise
    To heal the hurt and soothe the wrong.
For on the hill or in the dell,
    Or where the brook went leaping by
Or where the fields would surge and swell
    With golden wheat or bearded rye,
I felt her heart against my own,
    I breathed the sweetness of her breath,
Till all the cark of time had flown,
    And I was lord of life and death.

THE TEACHER

Lord, who am I to teach the way
To little children day by day,
So prone myself to go astray?

I teach them KNOWLEDGE, but I know
How faint they flicker and how low
The candles of my knowledge glow.

I teach them POWER to will and do,
But only now to learn anew
My own great weakness through and through.

I teach them LOVE for all mankind
And all God's creatures, but I find
My love comes lagging far behind.

Lord, if their guide I still must be,
Oh, let the little children see
The teacher leaning hard on Thee.

"SO QUIETLY"

NEWS *item from the* New York Times *on the lynching
of a Negro at Smithville, Ga., December 21, 1919:*
*"The train was boarded so quietly . . . that members
of the train crew did not know that the mob had seized the
Negro until informed by the prisoner's guard after the train
had left the town . . . A coroner's inquest held immedi-*

ately returned the verdict that West came to his death at
the hands of unidentified men."

So quietly they stole upon their prey
And dragged him out to death, so without flaw
Their black design, that they to whom the law
Gave him in keeping, in the broad, bright day,
Were not aware when he was snatched away;
And when the people, with a shrinking awe,
The horror of that mangled body saw,
"By unknown hands!" was all that they could say.

So, too, my country, stealeth on apace
The soul-blight of a nation. Not with drums
Or trumpet blare is that corruption sown,
But quietly—now in the open face
Of day, now in the dark—and when it comes,
Stern truth will never write, "By hands unknown."

ALEX ROGERS

ALEX ROGERS was born at Nashville, Tenn., in 1876, and was educated in the schools of that city. For many years he was a writer of words to popular songs. He wrote the lyrics for most of the songs in the muscial comedies in which Williams and Walker appeared. He also helped to construct and write the librettos and was responsible for much of the droll humor and many of the ludicrous situations in which they abounded. The verses of his herein included were originally written as texts for songs in those shows. He was also the author of the words of "The Jonah Man," "Nobody," "Bon Bon Buddy, the Chocolate Drop," and many other songs made popular by Bert Williams and George Walker. In later years he collaborated on Broadway musical plays and supplied "Negro stuff" for numbers of white performers. He died in New York, September 14, 1930.

WHY ADAM SINNED

"I heeard da ole folks talkin' in our house da other night
'Bout Adam in da scripchuh long ago.
Da lady folks all 'bused him, sed, "He knowed it wus'n right,"
An' 'cose da men folks dey all sed, "Dat's so."
I felt sorry fuh Mistuh Adam, an' I felt like puttin' in,
'Cause I knows mo' dan dey do, all 'bout whut made Adam sin:

Adam nevuh had no Mammy, fuh to take him on her knee
An' teach him right fum wrong an' show him

Things he ought to see.
I knows down in my heart—he'd-a let dat apple be
But Adam nevuh had no dear old Ma-am-my.

He nevuh knowed no chilehood roun' da ole log cabin do',
He nevuh knowed no pickaninny life.
He started in a great big grown up man, an' whut is mo',
He nevuh had da right kind uf a wife.
Jes s'pose he'd had a Mammy when dat temptin' did begin,
An' she'd a come an' tole him,
"Son, don' eat dat—dat's a sin."

But, Adam nevuh had no Mammy fuh to take him on her
knee
An' teach him right fum wrong an' show him
Things he ought to see.
I knows down in my heart he'd a let dat apple be,
But Adam nevuh had no dear old Ma-am-my.

THE RAIN SONG

Bro. Simmons
"Walk right in, Brother Wilson—how you feelin' today?"

Bro. Wilson
"Jes mod'rate, Brother Simmons, but den I ginnerly feels
dat way."

Bro. Simmons
"Here's White an' Black an' Brown an' Green; how's all
you gent'mens been?"

Bro. White
"My health is good but my bus'ness slack."

Bro. Black
"I'se been suff'rin' lots wid pains in my back."

Bro. Brown
"My ole 'ooman's sick, but I'se alright—"

Bro. Green
"Yes, I went aftuh Doctuh fuh her 'tuther night—"

Bro. Simmons
"Here's Sandy Turner, as I live!"

Bro. Turner
"Yes, I didn' 'spect to git here—but here I is!"

Bro. Simmons
"Now, gent'mens, make yo'selves to home,
Dare's nothin' to fear—my ole 'ooman's gone—
My stars; da weather's pow'ful warm—
I wouldn' be s'prised ef we had a storm."

Bro. Brown
"No, Brother Simmons, we kin safely say—
'Tain't gwine to be no storm today
Kase here am facts dat's mighty plain
An' any time you sees 'em you kin look fuh rain:
Any time you hears da cheers an' tables crack
An' da folks wid rheumatics—dare j'ints is on da rack—"

All

"Lookout fuh rain, rain rain.

"When da ducks quack loud an' da peacocks cry,
  An' da far off hills seems to be right nigh,
  Prepare fuh rain, rain, rain!

"When da ole cat on da hearth wid her velvet paws
  'Gins to wipin' over her whiskered jaws,
  Sho' sign o' rain, rain, rain!

"When da frog's done changed his yaller vest,
  An' in his brown suit he is dressed,
  Mo' rain, an' still mo' rain!

"When you notice da air it stan's stock still,
  An' da blackbird's voice it gits so awful shrill,
  Dat am da time fuh rain.

"When yo' dog quits bones an' begins to fas',
  An' when you see him eatin'; he's eatin' grass:
  Shoes', trues', cert'nes' sign ob rain!"

Refrain

"No, Brother Simmons, we kin safely say,
  'Tain't gwine tuh be no rain today,
  Kase da sut ain't fallin' an' da dogs ain't sleep,
  An' you ain't seen no spiders fum dare cobwebs creep;
  Las' night da sun went bright to bed,
  An' da moon ain't nevah once been seen to hang her head;
  If you'se watched all dis, den you kin safely say,
  Dat dare ain't a-gwine to be no rain today."

WAVERLY TURNER CARMICHAEL

WAVERLY TURNER CARMICHAEL *was born in Alabama. He attended the Snow Hill Institute in that state. While enrolled in one of the summer courses at Harvard University he brought a sheaf of his verses to the attention of one of the professors and was encouraged by him to publish them. His volume,* From the Heart of a Folk, *appeared in 1918. He served with the 367th Regiment, "The Buffaloes," during the World War, and saw active service in France.*

Carmichael is a disciple of Dunbar, and several of his efforts are merely clumsy paraphrases of certain of Dunbar's most popular poems. The pervading note in his thin volume is humility. His work is worthy of attention only because this humility is at times expressed with simple but compelling fervor.

KEEP ME, JESUS, KEEP ME

Keep me 'neath Thy mighty wing,
Keep me, Jesus, keep me;
Help me praise Thy Holy name,
Keep me, Jesus, keep me.
O my Lamb, come, my Lamb,
O my good Lamb,
Save me, Jesus, save me.

Hear me as I cry to Thee;
Keep me, Jesus, keep me;
May I that bright glory see;

Keep me, Jesus, keep me.
O my Lamb, my good Lamb,
O my good Lamb,
Keep me, Jesus, keep me.

WINTER IS COMING

De winter days are drawin' nigh
An' by the fire I sets an' sigh;
De no'the'n win' is blowin' cold,
Like it done in days of old.

De yaller leafs are fallin' fas',
Fur summer days is been an' pas';
The air is blowin' mighty cold,
Like it done in days of old.

De frost is fallin' on de gras'
An' seem to say, "Dis is yo' las' "—
De air is blowin' mighty cold
Like it done in days of old.

ALICE DUNBAR NELSON

A LICE DUNBAR NELSON *was born at New Orleans. She was educated in the schools of her native city, and has taken special courses at Cornell University, Columbia University and the University of Pennsylvania. In addition to uncollected poems, she is the author of these volumes of prose:* Violets and Other Tales (*1894*), The Goodness of St. Rocque (*1899*). *She edited* Masterpieces of Negro Eloquence (*1913*) *and the* Dunbar Speaker (*1920*). *Her first husband was Paul Laurence Dunbar, to whom she was married in 1898. She has been a teacher and is well known on the lecture platform and as a journalist.*

SONNET

I had no thought of violets of late,
The wild, shy kind that spring beneath your feet
In wistful April days, when lovers mate
And wander through the fields in raptures sweet.
The thought of violets meant florists' shops,
And bows and pins, and perfumed papers fine;
And garish lights, and mincing little fops
And cabarets and songs, and deadening wine.
So far from sweet real things my thoughts had strayed,
I had forgot wide fields, and clear brown streams;
The perfect loveliness that God has made,—
Wild violets shy and Heaven-mounting dreams.
And now—unwittingly, you've made me dream
Of violets, and my soul's forgotten gleam.

CLAUDE McKAY

CLAUDE MC KAY *was born in Jamaica, British West Indies. He received his education through being taught by an elder brother, who was a schoolmaster in one of the Jamaica villages. This elder brother was a strong influence in the formative years of McKay's life; he was a free-thinker and the possessor of a good library in which there were books by the great English scientists, novelists, and, above all, poets. The younger brother, by the time he was fourteen, had dipped into all these books and completely absorbed many of them. When he was nineteen he joined the Jamaica constabulary and served for almost a year. McKay in 1911, when he was twenty, published a volume of verse,* Songs of Jamaica. *Most of the poems in this collection were written in the Jamaican dialect. It is important to note that these dialect poems of McKay are quite distinct in sentiment and treatment from the conventional Negro dialect poetry written by the poets in the United States; they are free from both the minstrel and plantation traditions, free from exaggerated sweetness and wholesomeness; they are veritable impressions of Negro life in Jamaica. Indeed, some of these dialect poems are decidedly militant in tone. It is, of course, clear to see that McKay had the advantage of not having to deal with stereotypes. He found his medium fresh and plastic.*

These early poems were very popular in Jamaica, and their author became the Robert Burns of the island. In 1912 he was awarded the medal of the Institute of Arts and Sciences in recognition of his preëminence; he was the first Negro to receive this medal. In the same year he came to the United States to attend Tuskegee Institute. He remained at that school only a few months, later entering the Kansas State University, where he was for two years a student in the department of agriculture. He then came to New York, arriving in that city at just about the time that Harlem was beginning to assume form as the Negro world metropolis, and shortly abandoned all thought of returning to Jamaica. Between an unsuccessful investment in business and seeing life in New York he got rid of several thousand dollars—a legacy that had been left him. He then turned his hand to any sort of work he could find to earn a living. He worked as porter, houseman, longshoreman, barman, and waiter on dining-cars and in hotels. All the while he continued to write.

He first attracted attention in the United States by two sonnets, "The Harlem Dancer" and "Invocation," published in The Seven Arts in 1917, under the pseudonym, Eli Edwards. His poems then in quick succession began to appear in Pearson's, The Liberator, The Messenger, The Crisis, and other magazines. In 1920, while in London, he brought out Spring in New Hampshire, a volume of poems. In 1921 he was again in New York and became associate editor of The Liberator, of which Max Eastman was editor. In 1922 he published Harlem Shadows, his first volume to be brought out in the United States. In that same year he went to Russia, where he stayed six months. He has not been back to this country since, but has made his home most of the time in France.

McKay belongs to the post-war group and was its most powerful voice. He was preëminently the poet of rebellion. More effectively than any other poet of that period he voiced *the feelings and reactions the Negro in America was then experiencing. Incongruous as it may seem, he chose as the form of these poems of protest, challenge, and defiance the English sonnet; and no poetry in American literature sounds a more portentous note than these sonnet-tragedies. Read "The Lynching" and note particularly the final couplet:*

> And little lads, lynchers that were to be,
> Danced round the dreadful thing in fiendish glee.

The terrifying summer of 1919, when race riots occurred in quick succession in a dozen cities in different sections of the country, brought from him the most widely known of these sonnets, a cry of defiant desperation, beginning with the lines:

> If we must die—let it not be like hogs
> Hunted and penned in an inglorious spot,

and closing with:

> Like men we'll face the murderous, cowardly pack,
> Pressed to the wall, dying, but fighting back!

This is masculine poetry, strong and direct, the sort of poetry that stirs the pulse, that quickens to action. Reading McKay's poetry of protest and rebellion, it is difficult to imagine him dreaming of his native Jamaica and singing as he does in "Flame Heart" or creating poetic beauty in the absolute as he does in "The Harlem Dancer," "Spring in New Hampshire," and many another of his poems. Of the major Negro poets he, above all, is the poet of passion. That passion found in his poems of rebellion, transmuted, is felt in his love lyrics.

He was one of the principal forces in bringing about the Negro literary awakening. For the past five or six years he has been silent as a poet and has devoted himself to prose. In 1928 he published Home to Harlem, *a novel of Negro life in New York; this was followed by another novel,* Banjo, *in which the scene was laid in Marseilles.* Home to Harlem *gained for him the Harmon Gold Award for literature.*

THE LYNCHING

His spirit in smoke ascended to high heaven.
His father, by the cruelest way of pain,
Had bidden him to his bosom once again;
The awful sin remained still unforgiven.
All night a bright and solitary star
(Perchance the one that ever guided him,
Yet gave him up at last to Fate's wild whim)
Hung pitifully o'er the swinging char.
Day dawned, and soon the mixed crowds came to view
The ghastly body swaying in the sun:
The women thronged to look, but never a one
Showed sorrow in her eyes of steely blue;
And little lads, lynchers that were to be,
Danced round the dreadful thing in fiendish glee.

IF WE MUST DIE

If we must die—let it not be like hogs
Hunted and penned in an inglorious spot,
While round us bark the mad and hungry dogs,
Making their mock at our accursed lot.

If we must die—oh, let us nobly die,
So that our precious blood may not be shed
In vain; then even the monsters we defy
Shall be constrained to honor us though dead!
Oh, Kinsmen! We must meet the common foe;
Though far outnumbered, let us show us brave,
And for their thousand blows deal one death-blow!
What though before us lies the open grave?
Like men we'll face the murderous, cowardly pack,
Pressed to the wall, dying, but fighting back!

TO THE WHITE FIENDS

Think you I am not fiend and savage too?
Think you I could not arm me with a gun
And shoot down ten of you for every one
Of my black brothers murdered, burnt by you?
Be not deceived, for every deed you do
I could match—out-match: am I not Africa's son,
Black of that black land where black deeds are done?
But the Almighty from the darkness drew
My soul and said: Even thou shalt be a light
Awhile to burn on the benighted earth,
Thy dusky face I set among the white
For thee to prove thyself of highest worth;
Before the world is swallowed up in night,
To show thy little lamp: go forth, go forth!

THE HARLEM DANCER

Applauding youths laughed with young prostitutes
And watched her perfect, half-clothed body sway;

Her voice was like the sound of blended flutes
Blown by black players upon a picnic day.
She sang and danced on gracefully and calm,
The light gauze hanging loose about her form;
To me she seemed a proudly-swaying palm
Grown lovelier for passing through a storm.
Upon her swarthy neck black, shiny curls
Profusely fell; and, tossing coins in praise,
The wine-flushed, bold-eyed boys, and even the girls,
Devoured her with their eager, passionate gaze;
But looking at her falsely-smiling face,
I knew her self was not in that strange place.

HARLEM SHADOWS

I hear the halting footsteps of a lass
    In Negro Harlem when the night lets fall
Its veil. I see the shapes of girls who pass
    To bend and barter at desire's call.
Ah, little dark girls, who in slippered feet
    Go prowling through the night from street to street!

Through the long night until the silver break
    Of day the little gray feet know no rest;
Through the lone night until the last snow-flake
    Has dropped from heaven upon the earth's white breast,
The dusky, half-clad girls of tired feet
    Are trudging, thinly shod, from street to street.

Ah, stern harsh world, that in the wretched way
    Of poverty, dishonor and disgrace,
Has pushed the timid little feet of clay,
    The sacred brown feet of my fallen race!

Ah, heart of me, the weary, weary feet
  'In Harlem wandering from street to street.

AFTER THE WINTER

Some day, when trees have shed their leaves
  And against the morning's white
The shivering birds beneath the eaves
  Have sheltered for the night,
We'll turn our faces southward, love,
  Toward the summer isle
Where bamboos spire the shafted grove
  And wide-mouthed orchids smile.

And we will seek the quiet hill
  Where towers the cotton tree,
And leaps the laughing crystal rill,
  And works the droning bee.
And we will build a cottage there
  Beside an open glade,
With black-ribbed bluebells blowing near,
  And ferns that never fade.

SPRING IN NEW HAMPSHIRE

Too green the springing April grass,
Too blue the silver-speckled sky,
For me to linger here, alas,
While happy winds go laughing by,
Wasting the golden hours indoors,
Washing windows and scrubbing floors.

Too wonderful the April night,
Too faintly sweet the first May flowers,
The stars too gloriously bright,
For me to spend the evening hours,
When fields are fresh and streams are leaping,
Wearied, exhausted, dully sleeping.

THE TIRED WORKER

O whisper, O my soul! The afternoon
Is waning into evening, whisper soft!
Peace, O my rebel heart! for soon the moon
From out its misty veil will swing aloft!
Be patient, weary body, soon the night
Will wrap thee gently in her sable sheet,
And with a leaden sigh thou wilt invite
To rest thy tired hands and aching feet.
The wretched day was theirs, the night is mine;
Come, tender sleep, and fold me to thy breast.
But what steals out the gray clouds red like wine?
O dawn! O dreaded dawn! O let me rest!
Weary my veins, my brain, my life! Have pity!
No! Once again the harsh, the ugly city.

THE BARRIER

I must not gaze at them although
    Your eyes are dawning day;
I must not watch you as you go
    Your sun-illumined way;

I hear but I must never heed
   The fascinating note,
Which, fluting like a river-reed,
   Comes from your trembling throat;

I must not see upon your face
   Love's softly glowing spark;
For there's the barrier of race,
   You're fair and I am dark.

TO O. E. A.

Your voice is the color of a robin's breast,
   And there's a sweet sob in it like rain—still rain in the
      night.
Among the leaves of the trumpet-tree, close to his nest,
   The pea-dove sings, and each note thrills me with strange
      delight
Like the words, wet with music, that well from your trem-
   bling throat.
     I'm afraid of your eyes, they're so bold,
     Searching me through, reading my thoughts, shining
      like gold.
But sometimes they are gentle and soft like the dew on
   the lips of the eucharis
Before the sun comes warm with his lover's kiss.
   You are sea-foam, pure with the star's loveliness,
Not mortal, a flower, a fairy, too fair for the beauty-shorn
   earth.
All wonderful things, all beautiful things, gave of their
   wealth to your birth:

O I love you so much, not recking of passion, that I feel
    it is wrong!
But men will love you, flower, fairy, non-mortal spirit
    burdened with flesh,
Forever, life-long.

FLAME-HEART

So much have I forgotten in ten years,
    So much in ten brief years! I have forgot
What time the purple apples come to juice,
    And what month brings the shy forget-me-not.
I have forgot the special, startling season
    Of the pimento's flowering and fruiting,
What time of year the ground doves brown the fields
    And fill the noonday with their curious fluting.
I have forgotten much, but still remember
The poinsettia's red, blood-red in warm December.

I still recall the honey-fever grass,
    But cannot recollect the high days when
We rooted them out of the ping-wing path
    To stop the mad bees in the rabbit pen.
I often try to think in what sweet month
    The languid painted ladies used to dapple
The yellow bye road mazing from the main,
    Sweet with the golden threads of the rose-apple.
I have forgotten—strange—but quite remember
The poinsettia's red, blood-red in warm December.

What weeks, what months, what time of the mild year
    We cheated school to have our fling at tops?

What days our wine-thrilled bodies pulsed with joy
   Feasting upon blackberries in the copse?
Oh, some I know! I have embalmed the days,
   Even the sacred moments, when we played,
All innocent of passion uncorrupt,
   At noon and evening in the flame-heart's shade.
We were so happy, happy—I remember
Beneath the poinsettia's red in warm December.

COMMEMORATION

When first your glory shone upon my face
   My body kindled to a mighty flame,
And burnt you yielding in my hot embrace
   Until you swooned to love, breathing my name.

And wonder came and filled our night of sleep,
   Like a new comet crimsoning the sky;
And stillness like the stillness of the deep
   Suspended lay as an unuttered sigh.

I never again shall feel your warm heart flushed,
   Panting with passion, naked unto mine,
Until the throbbing world around is hushed
   To quiet worship at our scented shrine.

Nor will your glory seek my swarthy face,
   To kindle and to change my jaded frame
Into a miracle of godlike grace,
   Transfigured, bathed in your immortal flame.

TWO-AN'-SIX

Merry voices chatterin',
Nimble feet dem patterin',
Big an' little, faces gay,
Happy day dis market day.

Sateday, de marnin' break,
Soon, soon market-people wake;
An' de light shine from de moon
While dem boy, wid pantaloon
Roll up ober dem knee-pan,
'Tep across de buccra lan'
To de pastur whe' de harse
Feed along wid de jackass,
An' de mule cant' in de track
Wid him tail up in him back,
All de ketchin' to defy,
No ca' how dem boy might try.

In de early marnin'-tide,
When de cocks crow on de hill
An' de stars are shinin' still,
Mirrie by de fireside
Hots de coffee for de lads
Comin' ridin' on de pads
T'rown across dem animul—
Donkey, harse too, an' de mule,
Which at last had come do'n cool.
On de bit dem hol' dem full:
Racin' ober pastur' lan',
See dem comin' ebery man,

Comin' fe de steamin' tea
Ober hilly track an' lea.

Hard-wuk'd donkey on de road
Trottin' wid him ushal load,
Hamper pack' wi' yam an' grain,
Sour-sop, and Gub'nor cane.

Cous' Sun sits in hired dray,
Drivin' 'long de market way;
Whole week grindin' sugar cane
T'rough de boilin' sun an' rain,
Now, a'ter de toilin' hard,
He goes seekin' his reward,
While he's thinkin' in him min'
Of de dear ones lef' behin',
Of de loved though ailin' wife,
Darlin' treasure of his life,
An' de picknies, six in all,
Whose 'nuff burdens 'pon him fall:
Seben lovin' ones in need,
Seben hungry mouths fe feed;
On deir wants he thinks alone,
Neber dreamin' of his own,
But gwin' on wid joyful face
Till him re'ch de market-place.

Sugar bears no price today,
Though it is de mont' o' May,
When de time is hellish hot,
An' de water cocoanut
An' de cane bebridge is nice,
Mix' up wid a lilly ice.

Big an' little, great an' small,
Afou yam is all de call;
Sugar tup an' gill a quart,
Yet de people hab de heart
Wantin' brater top o' i',
Want de sweatin' higgler fe
Ram de pan an' pile i' up,
Yet sell i' fe so-so tup.

Cousin Sun is lookin' sad,
As de market is so bad;
'Pon him han' him res' him chin,
Quietly sit do'n thinkin'
Of de loved wife sick in bed,
An' de children to be fed—
What de laborers would say
When dem know him couldn' pay;
Also what about de mill
Whe' him hire from old Bill;
So him think, an' think on so,
Till him t'oughts no more could go.

Then he got up an' began
Pickin' up him sugar-pan:
In his ears rang t'rough de din
"Only two-an'-six a tin'."
What a tale he'd got to tell,
How bad, bad de sugar sell!
Tekin' out de lee amount,
Him set do'n an' begin count
All de time him min' deh doubt
How expenses would pay out;

Ah, it gnawed him like de ticks,
Sugar sell fe two-an'-six!

So he journeys on de way,
Feelin' sad dis market day;
No e'en buy a little cake
To gi'e baby when she wake—
Passin' 'long de candy-shop
'Douten eben mek a stop
To buy drops fe las'y son,
For de lilly cash nea' done.
So him re'ch him own a groun',
An' de children scamper roun',
Each one stretchin' out him han',
Lookin' to de poor, sad man.

Oh, how much he felt de blow,
As he watched dem face fall low,
When dem wait an' nuttin' came,
An' drew back deir han's wid shame!
But de sick wife kissed his brow:
"Sun, don't get down-hearted now;
Ef we only pay expense
We mus' wuk we common-sense,
Cut an' carve, an' carve an' cut,
Mek gill sarbe fe quattiewut;
We mus' try mek two ends meet
Neber mind how hard be it.
We won't mind de haul an' pull,
While dem pickny belly full."

An' de shadow lef' him face,
An' him felt an inward peace,

As he blessed his better part
For her sweet an' gentle heart:
"Dear one o' my heart, my breat',
Won't I lub you to de deat'?
When my heart is weak an' sad,
Who but you can mek it glad?"

So dey kissed an' kissed again,
An' deir t'oughts were not on pain,
But was 'way down in de sout'
Where dey'd wedded in deir yout',
In de marnin' of deir life
Free from all de grief an' strife,
Happy in de marnin' light,
Never thinkin' of de night.

So dey k'lated eberyt'ing;
An' de profit it could bring,
A'ter all de business fix',
Was a princely two-an'-six.

GEORGIA DOUGLAS JOHNSON

GEORGIA DOUGLAS JOHNSON *was born in Atlanta, Ga.*
*She was educated in the public schools of that city and
at Atlanta University. She was the first colored woman after
Frances Harper to gain general recognition as a poet. Mrs.
Johnson is purely a lyrist; she sings the emotions. Her song
is not novel, nor does it display a wide range; it is based
on age-old themes, and the treatment is conventional. It is
not difficult to find in her work an obviousness in technique
and a triteness of philosophy, but it also contains the sincere
simplicity that carries conviction. It may be that her verse
possesses effectiveness precisely because it is at the pole oppo-
site to adroitness, sophistication, and a jejune pretention to
metaphysics. Her poems are songs of the heart, written to
appeal to the heart. In point of time she belongs with the
immediate post-war group, and a number of her poems were
poems of protest.*

Mrs. Johnson is the author of three volumes of poetry:
The Heart of a Woman (*1918*), Bronze (*1922*), *and* An
Autumn Love Cycle (*1928*). *She lives in Washington, and
her home has long been a center for the Negro literary group
of the city.*

THE HEART OF A WOMAN

The heart of a woman goes forth with the dawn,
As a lone bird, soft winging, so restlessly on,
Afar o'er life's turrets and vales does it roam
In the wake of those echoes the heart calls home.

The heart of a woman falls back with the night,
And enters some alien cage in its plight,
And tries to forget it has dreamed of the stars,
While it breaks, breaks, breaks on the sheltering bars.

YOUTH

The dew is on the grasses, dear,
   The blush is on the rose,
And swift across our dial-youth,
   A shifting shadow goes.

The primrose moments, lush with bliss,
   Exhale and fade away,
Life may renew the Autumn time,
   But nevermore the May!

LOST ILLUSIONS

Oh, for the veils of my far away youth,
Shielding my heart from the blaze of the truth,
Why did I stray from their shelter and grow
Into the sadness that follows—to know!

Impotent atom with desolate gaze
Threading the tumult of hazardous ways—
Oh, for the veils, for the veils of my youth
Veils that hung low o'er the blaze of the truth!

I WANT TO DIE WHILE YOU LOVE ME

I want to die while you love me,
    While yet you hold me fair,
While laughter lies upon my lips
    And lights are in my hair.

I want to die while you love me,
    And bear to that still bed,
Your kisses turbulent, unspent,
    To warm me when I'm dead.

I want to die while you love me,
    Oh, who would care to live
Till love has nothing more to ask
    And nothing more to give!

I want to die while you love me
    And never, never see
The glory of this perfect day
    Grow dim or cease to be.

WELT

Would I might mend the fabric of my youth
That daily flaunts its tatters to my eyes,
Would I might compromise awhile with truth
Until our moon now waxing, wanes and dies.

For I would go a further while with you,
And drain this cup so tantalant and fair
Which meets my parchèd lips like cooling dew,
Ere time has brushed cold fingers through my hair!

MY LITTLE DREAMS

I'm folding up my little dreams
Within my heart tonight,
And praying I may soon forget
The torture of their sight.

For Time's deft fingers scroll my brow
With fell relentless art—
I'm folding up my little dreams
Tonight, within my heart!

JOSEPH SEAMON COTTER, JR.

JOSEPH SEAMON COTTER, JR., *was born at Louisville, Kentucky, September 2, 1895. He was a precocious child and read a number of books before he was six years old. Through his boyhood he had the advantages of a full library and the encouragement of his father, himself a writer. Young Cotter attended Fisk University but left in his second year because he had developed tuberculosis. Most of his poems he wrote during the six years of his illness, beginning in 1913. But his best work places him in the post-war class of Negro poets and ranks him high among them. These later poems reveal a sensitive imagination and delicate workmanship; at the same time, their texture is firm. "And What Shall You Say?" was a much-quoted poem immediately following the war.*

The promise that Cotter gave was not allowed to reach fulfillment. He died in 1919 at the age of twenty-four. He published a collection of poems, The Band of Gideon, *in 1918. This is a volume of less than thirty pages, but it assays an uncommonly high percentage of genuine poetry.*

A PRAYER

As I lie in bed,
Flat on my back;
There passes across my ceiling
An endless panorama of things—
Quick steps of gay-voiced children,
Adolescence in its wondering silences,

185

Maid and man on moonlit summer's eve,
Women in the holy glow of Motherhood,
Old men gazing silently through the twilight
Into the beyond.
O God, give me words to make my dream-children live.

AND WHAT SHALL YOU SAY?

Brother, come!
And let us go unto our God.
And when we stand before Him
I shall say—
"Lord, I do not hate,
I am hated.
I scourge no one,
I am scourged.
I covet no lands,
My lands are coveted.
I mock no peoples,
My people are mocked."
And, brother, what shall you say?

IS IT BECAUSE I AM BLACK?

Why do men smile when I speak,
And call my speech
The whimperings of a babe
That cries but knows not what it wants?
Is it because I am black?

Why do men sneer when I arise
And stand in their councils,

And look them eye to eye,
And speak their tongue?
Is it because I am black?

THE BAND OF GIDEON

The band of Gideon roam the sky,
The howling wind is their war-cry,
The thunder's roll is their trump's peal,
And the lightning's flash their vengeful steel.
  Each black cloud
  Is a fiery steed.
  And they cry aloud
  With each strong deed,
"The sword of the Lord and Gideon."

And men below rear temples high
And mock their God with reasons why,
And live in arrogance, sin and shame,
And rape their souls for the world's good name.
  Each black cloud
  Is a fiery steed.
  And they cry aloud
  With each strong deed,
"The sword of the Lord and Gideon."

The band of Gideon roam the sky
And view the earth with baleful eye;
In holy wrath they scourge the land
With earthquake, storm and burning brand.

Each black cloud
Is a fiery steed.
And they cry aloud
With each strong deed,
"The sword of the Lord and Gideon."

The lightnings flash and the thunders roll,
And "Lord have mercy on my soul,"
Cry men as they fall on the stricken sod,
In agony searching for their God.
Each black cloud
Is a fiery steed.
And they cry aloud
With each strong deed,
"The sword of the Lord and Gideon."

And men repent and then forget
That heavenly wrath they ever met,
The band of Gideon yet will come
And strike their tongues of blasphemy dumb.
Each black cloud
Is a fiery steed.
And they cry aloud
With each strong deed,
"The sword of the Lord and Gideon."

RAIN MUSIC

On the dusty earth-drum
Beats the falling rain;
Now a whispered murmur,
Now a louder strain.

Slender, silvery drumsticks,
   On an ancient drum,
Beat the mellow music
   Bidding life to come.

Chords of earth awakened,
   Notes of greening spring,
Rise and fall triumphant
   Over every thing.

Slender, silvery drumsticks
   Beat the long tattoo—
God, the Great Musician,
   Calling life anew.

SUPPLICATION

I am so tired and weary,
   So tired of the endless fight,
So weary of waiting the dawn
   And finding endless night.

That I ask but rest and quiet—
   Rest for days that are gone,
And quiet for the little space
   That I must journey on.

RAY GARFIELD DANDRIDGE

RAY GARFIELD DANDRIDGE *was born at Cincinnati in 1882 and educated in the schools of that city. In 1912, as the result of a stroke of paralysis he lost the use of both legs and his right arm. He wrote most of his poems in an invalid's bed. He was a disciple of Dunbar, but it is interesting to compare his "Zalka Peetruza," beyond question the best of all his poems, with McKay's "The Harlem Dancer."* He published two volumes, The Poet and Other Poems *(1920) and* Zalka Peetruza and Other Poems *(1928). He died in 1930.*

TIME TO DIE

Black brother, think you life so sweet
That you would live at any price?
Does mere existence balance with
The weight of your great sacrifice?
Or can it be you fear the grave
Enough to live and die a slave?
O Brother! be it better said,
When you are gone and tears are shed,
That your death was the stepping stone
Your children's children cross'd upon.
Men have died that men might live:
Look every foeman in the eye!
If necessary, your life give
For something, ere in vain you die.

'ITTLE TOUZLE HEAD

(*To R. V. P.*)

Cum, listen w'ile yore Unkel sings
Erbout how low sweet chariot swings,
Truint Angel, wifout wings,
Mah 'ittle Touzle Head.

Stop! Stop! How dare you laff et me,
Bekaze I foul de time an' key,
Thinks you dat I is Black Pattie,
Mah 'ittle Touzle Head?

O, Honey Lam'! dem sparklin' eyes,
Dat offen laffs an' selem cries,
Is sho a God gib natchel prize,
Mah 'ittle Touzle Head.

An' doze wee han's so sof' an' sweet,
Mates wid dem toddlin', velvet feet,
Jes to roun' you out, complete,
Mah 'ittle Touzle Head.

Sma't! youse sma't ez sma't kin be,
Knows yore evah A, B, C,
Plum on down to X, Y, Z,
Mah 'ittle Touzle Head.

De man doan know how much he miss,
Ef he ain't got no niece lak dis;
Fro yore Unkel one mo' kiss,
Mah 'ittle Touzle Head!

I wist sum magic w'u'd ellow,
(By charm or craf'—doan mattah how)
You stay jes lak you is right now,
Mah 'ittle Touzle Head.

ZALKA PEETRUZA

(*Who Was Christened Lucy Jane*)

She danced, near nude, to tom-tom beat,
With swaying arms and flying feet,
'Mid swirling spangles, gauze and lace,
Her all was dancing—save her face.

A conscience, dumb to brooding fears,
Companioned hearing deaf to cheers;
A body, marshaled by the will,
Kept dancing while a heart stood still:

And eyes obsessed with vacant stare,
Looked over heads to empty air,
As though they sought to find therein
Redemption for a maiden sin.

'Twas thus, amid force driven grace,
We found the lost look on her face;
And then, to us, did it occur
That, though we saw—we saw not her.

SPRIN' FEVAH

Dar's a lazy, sortah hazy
Feelin' grips me, thoo an' thoo;

An' I feels lak doin' less dan enythin';
Dough de saw is sharp an' greasy,
Dough de task et han' is easy,
An' de day am fair an' breezy,
Dar's a thief dat steals embition in de win'.

Kaint defy it, kaint deny it,
Kaze it jes won't be denied;
It's a mos' pursistin' stubbern sortah thin';
Anti Tox' doan neutrolize it;
Doctahs fail to analyze it;
So I yiel's (dough I despise it)
To dat res'less, wretchit fevah evah Sprin'.

DE DRUM MAJAH

He's struttin' sho ernuff,
Wearin' a lady's muff
En' ways erpon his head,
Red coat ob reddest red,
Purtty white satin ves',
Gole braid ercross de ches';
Goo'ness! he cuts a stunt,
Prancin' out dar in frunt,
      Leadin' his ban'.

W'en dat ah whistle blows,
Each man behine him knows
'Zacklee whut he mus' do;
You bet! he dues it, too.
W'en dat brass stick he twirls,
Ole maids an' lub-sick gurls

Looks on wid longin' eyes,
Dey simply idolize
   Dat han'sum man.

Sweet fife an' piccalo,
Bofe warblin' sof' an' lo',
Slide ho'n an' saxophones,
Jazz syncopated tones,
Snare drum an' lead cornet,
Alto an' clarinet,
Las', but not least, dar cum
Cymbals an' big bass drum—
   O! whut a ban'!

Cose, we all undahstan'
Each piece he'ps maik de ban',
But dey all mus' be led,
Sum one mus' be de head:
No doubt, de centipede
Has all de laigs he need,
But take erway de head,
Po' centipede am dead;
   So am de ban'.

ROSCOE CONKLING JAMISON

R OSCOE CONKLING JAMISON *belongs to the post-war group of poets. His "The Negro Soldiers" stands so far above everything else he wrote that he falls also into the class of poets of one poem. He was born in Winchester, Tenn., 1888. He died in 1918.*

THE NEGRO SOLDIERS

These truly are the Brave,
These men who cast aside
Old memories, to walk the blood-stained pave
Of Sacrifice, joining the solemn tide
That moves away, to suffer and to die
For Freedom—when their own is yet denied!
O Pride! O Prejudice! When they pass by,
Hail them, the Brave, for you now crucified!

These truly are the Free,
These souls that grandly rise
Above base dreams of vengeance for their wrongs,
Who march to war with visions in their eyes
Of Peace through Brotherhood, lifting glad songs,
Aforetime, while they front the firing line.
Stand and behold! They take the field today,
Shedding their blood like Him now held divine,
That those who mock might find a better way!

R. NATHANIEL DETT

R. NATHANIEL DETT *was born in Drummondville, Canada, in 1882. He is a graduate of the Oberlin Conservatory of Music and is a composer of note. Most of his compositions are based on Negro folk themes. He is director of music at Hampton Institute. He is the author of* The Album of a Heart, *a volume of verse.*

THE RUBINSTEIN STACCATO ETUDE

Staccato! Staccato!
Leggier agitato!
 In and out does the melody twist—
Unique proposition
Is this composition.
 (Alas! for the player who hasn't the wrist!)
Now in the dominant
Theme ringing prominent,
 Bass still repeating its one monotone,
Double notes crying,
Up keyboard go flying,
 The change to the minor comes in like a groan.
Without a cessation
A chaste modulation
 Hastens adown to subdominant key,
Where melody mellow-like
Singing so 'cello-like
 Rises and falls in a wild ecstasy.

Scarce is this finished
When chords all diminished
    Break loose in a patter that comes down like rain;
A pedal-point wonder
Rivaling thunder,
    Now all is mad agitation again.
Like laughter jolly
Begins the finale;
    Again does the 'cello its tones seem to lend
Diminuendo ad molto crescendo.
    Ah! Rubinstein only could make such an end!

CHARLES BERTRAM JOHNSON

CHARLES BERTRAM JOHNSON *was born in Callao, Mo.,
1880. He was educated in the public schools of his
native town and at Western College, Lincoln Institute, and
Chicago University. He was a teacher for a while and later
entered the ministry. He is the author of two pamphlets of
poetry,* Wind Whisperings (*1900*) *and* The Mantle of
Dunbar (*1918*), *and of one volume,* Songs of My People
(*1918*). *His work is respectable, not varying in any great
degree either up or down from that level.*

A LITTLE CABIN

Des a little cabin
Big ernuff fur two.
Des awaitin', honey,
Cozy fixt fur you;
Down dah by de road,
Not ve'y far from town,
Waitin' fur de missis,
When she's ready to come down.

Des a little cabin,
An' er acre o' groun',
Vines agrowin' on it,
Fruit trees all aroun',
Hollyhawks a-bloomin'
In de gyahden plot—
Honey, would you like to
Own dat little spot?

198

Make dat little cabin
Cheery, clean an' bright,
With an' angel in it
Like a ray of light?
Make dat little palace
Somethin' fine an' gran',
Make it like an Eden,
Fur a lonely man?

Des you listen, Honey,
While I 'splain it all,
How some lady's go'nter
Boss dat little hall;
Des you take my han'
Dat's de way it's writ,
Des you take my heart,
Dat's de deed to it.

NEGRO POETS

Full many lift and sing
Their sweet imagining;
Not yet the Lyric Seer,
The one bard of the throng,
With highest gift of song,
Breaks on our sentient ear.

Not yet the gifted child,
With notes enraptured, wild,
That storm and throng the heart,
To make his rage our own,
Our hearts his lyric throne;
Hard won by cosmic art.

I hear the sad refrain,
Of slavery's sorrow-strain;
The broken half-lispt speech
Of freedom's twilit hour;
The greater growing reach
Of larger latent power.

Here and there a growing note
Swells from a conscious throat;
Thrilled with a message fraught
The pregnant hour is near;
We wait our Lyric Seer;
By whom our wills are caught.

Who makes our cause and wrong
The motif of his song;
Who sings our racial good,
Bestows us honor's place,
The cosmic brotherhood
Of genius—not of race.

Blind Homer, Greek or Jew,
Of fame's immortal few
Would still be deathless born;
Frail Dunbar, black or white,
In Fame's eternal light,
Would shine a Star of Morn.

An unhorizoned range,
Our hour of doubt and change,
Gives song a nightless day,
Whose pen with pregnant mirth
Will give our longings birth,
And point our souls the way?

JOSHUA HENRY JONES

JOSHUA HENRY JONES *was born at Orangeburg, South Carolina. After his graduation from Brown University he went into newspaper work. Beginning on the Providence* News, *he has worked on a number of New England newspapers. He has been city editor of the Boston* Advertiser *and has been employed in various editorial capacities on several other Boston dailies. He was for four years secretary to Mayor James M. Curley of Boston, by whom he was appointed editor of the* City Record. *Mr. Jones is the author of* The Heart of the World and Other Poems, Poems of the Four Seas, *and* By Sanction of Law, *a novel.*

TO A SKULL

Ghastly, ghoulish, grinning skull,
Toothless, eyeless, hollow, dull,
Why your smirk and empty smile
As the hours away you while?
Has the earth become such bore
That it pleases nevermore?
Whence your joy through sun and rain?
Is 't because of loss of pain?
Have you learned what men learn not
That earth's substance turns to rot?
After learning now you scan
Vain endeavors man by man?
Do you mind that you as they
Once were held by mystic sway;

Dreamed and struggled, hoped and prayed,
Lolled and with the minutes played?
Sighed for honors; battles planned;
Sipped of cups that wisdom banned
But would please the weak frail flesh;
Suffered, fell, 'rose, struggled fresh?
Now that you are but a skull
Glimpse your life as life is, full
Of beauties that we miss
Till time withers with his kiss?
Do you laugh in cynic vein
Since you cannot try again?
And you know that we, like you,
Will too late our failings rue?
Tell me, ghoulish, grinning skull
What deep broodings o'er you mull?
Tell me why you smirk and smile
Ere I pass life's sunset stile.

OTTO LELAND BOHANAN

OTTO LELAND BOHANAN *was born in Washington. He attended the public schools there and was graduated from Howard University. Later he did special work at the Catholic University. Later he came to New York and engaged in the musical profession. His poems have appeared in many periodicals.*

THE DAWN'S AWAKE!

The Dawn's awake!
  A flash of smoldering flame and fire
Ignites the East. Then, higher, higher,
    O'er all the sky so gray, forlorn,
    The torch of gold is borne.

The Dawn's awake!
  . The dawn of a thousand dreams and thrills.
And music singing in the hills
    A paean of eternal spring
    Voices the new awakening.

The Dawn's awake!
  Whispers of pent-up harmonies,
With the mingled fragrance of the trees;
    Faint snatches of half-forgotten song—
    Fathers! torn and numb—
      The boon of light we craved, awaited long,
    Has come, has come!

THE WASHER-WOMAN

A great swart cheek and the gleam of tears,
The flutter of hopes and the shadow of fears,
And all day long the rub and scrub
With only a breath betwixt tub and tub.
Fool! Thou hast toiled for fifty years
And what hast thou now but thy dusty tears?
In silence she rubbed . . . But her face I had seen,
Where the light of her soul fell shining and clean.

JESSIE REDMOND FAUSET

JESSIE REDMOND FAUSET *was born at Snow Hill, N. J. She was educated in the public schools of Philadelphia and at Cornell University and the University of Pennsylvania. She was for some years a teacher of Latin and French in the Dunbar High School at Washington. She is the author of a number of uncollected poems and of two novels:* There Is Confusion *(1924) and* Plum Bun *(1929). Her touch is light and neat, and may be seen at its best in the* vers de société *that she has written. She has made skillful translations from the French of some of the Negro poets of the French West Indies. Miss Fauset was for several years the literary editor of* The Crisis. *She is now a teacher of French in the New York public schools.*

LA VIE C'EST LA VIE

On summer afternoons I sit
Quiescent by you in the park,
And idly watch the sunbeams gild
And tint the ash-trees' bark.

Or else I watch the squirrels frisk
And chaffer in the grassy lane;
And all the while I mark your voice
Breaking with love and pain.

I know a woman who would give
Her chance of heaven to take my place;

To see the love-light in your eyes,
The love-glow on your face!

And there's a man whose lightest word
Can set my chilly blood afire;
Fulfillment of his least behest
Defines my life's desire.

But he will none of me, nor I
Of you. Nor you of her. 'Tis said
The world is full of jests like these.—
I wish that I were dead.

CHRISTMAS EVE IN FRANCE

Oh, little Christ, why do you sigh
    As you look down tonight
On breathless France, on bleeding France,
    And all her dreadful plight?
What bows your childish head so low?
    What turns your cheek so white?

Oh, little Christ, why do you moan,
    What is it that you see
In mourning France, in martyred France,
    And her great agony?
Does she recall your own dark day,
    Your own Gethsemane?

Oh, little Christ, why do you weep,
    Why flow your tears so sore
For pleading France, for praying France,
    A suppliant at God's door?

"God sweetened not my cup," you say,
  "Shall He for France do more?"

Oh, little Christ, what can this mean,
  Why must this horror be
For fainting France, for faithful France,
  And her sweet chivalry?
"I bled to free all men," you say,
  "France bleeds to keep men free."

Oh, little, lovely Christ—you smile!
  What guerdon is in store
For gallant France, for glorious France,
  And all her valiant corps?
"Behold I live, and France, like me,
  Shall live for evermore."

DEAD FIRES

If this is peace, this dead and leaden thing,
  Then better far the hateful fret, the sting.
Better the wound forever seeking balm
  Than this gray calm!

Is this pain's surcease? Better far the ache,
  The long-drawn dreary day, the night's white wake,
Better the choking sigh, the sobbing breath
  Than passion's death!

ORIFLAMME

"I can remember when I was a little, young girl, how my old
mammy would sit out of doors in the evenings and look up at

the stars and groan, and I would say, 'Mammy, what makes you groan so?' And she would say, 'I am groaning to think of my poor children; they do not know where I be and I don't know where they be. I look up at the stars and they look up at the stars!' "—*Sojourner Truth.*

I think I see her sitting bowed and black,
  Stricken and seared with slavery's mortal scars,
Reft of her children, lonely, anguished, yet
  Still looking at the stars.

Symbolic mother, we thy myriad sons,
  Pounding our stubborn hearts on Freedom's bars,
Clutching our birthright, fight with faces set,
  Still visioning the stars!

OBLIVION

From the French of Massillon Coicou (*Haiti*)

I hope when I am dead that I shall lie
  In some deserted grave—I cannot tell you why,
But I should like to sleep in some neglected spot,
  Unknown to every one, by every one forgot.

There lying I should taste with my dead breath
  The utter lack of life, the fullest sense of death;
And I should never hear the note of jealousy or hate,
  The tribute paid by passers-by to tombs of state.

To me would never penetrate the prayers and tears
  That futilely bring torture to dead and dying ears;
There I should lie annihilate and my dead heart would bless
  Oblivion—the shroud and envelope of happiness.

THEODORE HENRY SHACKLEFORD

THEODORE HENRY SHACKLEFORD *was born in Windsor, Canada, in 1888, the grandson of escaped slaves. He received his education in the United States, at the Downingtown Industrial Training School, Downington, Pa. He pub-lished two volumes of poetry,* Mammy's Cracklin' Bread *and* My Country and Other Poems *(1918). The selection that follows is from the latter volume. He died in Jamaica, N.Y., in 1923.*

THE BIG BELL IN ZION

Come, children, hear the joyful sound,
    Ding, Dong, Ding.
Go spread the glad news all around,
    Ding, Dong, Ding.

Chorus
Oh, the big bell's tollin' up in Zion,
    The big bell's tollin' up in Zion,
    The big bell's tollin' up in Zion,
      Ding, Dong, Ding.

I've been abused and tossed about,
    Ding, Dong, Ding!
But glory to the Lamb! I shout,
    Ding, Dong, Ding!

My bruthah jus' sent word to me,
　　Ding, Dong, Ding.
That he'd done set his own self free.
　　Ding, Dong, Ding.

Ole massa said he could not go,
　　Ding, Dong, Ding.
But he's done reached Ohio sho'.
　　Ding, Dong, Ding.

Ise gwine to be real nice an' meek,
　　Ding, Dong, Ding.
Den I'll run away myself nex' week.
　　Ding, Dong, Ding.

Chorus
Oh, the big bell's tollin' up in Zion,
　　The big bell's tollin' up in Zion,
　　The big bell's tollin' up in Zion,
　　　Ding, Dong, Ding.

LUCIAN B. WATKINS

LUCIAN B. WATKINS *was born in Chesterfield, Va., 1879. He was educated in the public schools of his native town and at the Virginia Normal and Industrial Institute, Petersburg, and began active life as a teacher. He served overseas in the World War and lost his health. He died in Fort Mercury Hospital in 1921. He is the author of* Voices of Solitude (*1907*). *A number of his poems are spirited in tone.*

STAR OF ETHIOPIA

Out in the Night thou art the sun
Toward which thy soul-charmed children run,
    The faith-high height whereon they see
    The glory of their Day To Be—
The peace at last when all is done.

The night is dark but, one by one,
Thy signals, ever and anon,
    Smile beacon answers to their plea,
    Out in the Night.

Ah, Life! thy storms these cannot shun;
Give them a hope to rest upon,
    A dream to dream eternally,
    The strength of men who would be free
And win the battle race begun,
    Out in the Night!

TWO POINTS OF VIEW

From this low-lying valley, oh, how sweet
And cool and calm and great is life, I ween,
There on yon mountain-throne—that sun-gold crest!

From this uplifted, mighty mountain-seat,
How bright and still and warm and soft and green
Seems yon low lily-vale of peace and rest!

TO OUR FRIENDS

We've kept the faith. Our souls' high dreams
    Untouched by bondage and its rod,
Burn on! and on! and on! It seems
    We shall have FRIENDS—while God is God!

ANNE SPENCER

A NNE SPENCER *was born in Bramwell, West Virginia, 1882. She was educated at the Virginia Seminary in Lynchburg. Her position is unique among Aframerican poets; she is the first woman to show so high a degree of maturity in what she wrote. There is an absence of juvenility in her work. She is less obvious and less subjective than any of her predecessors and most of her contemporaries. Economy of phrase and compression of thought are, perhaps, more characteristic of her than of any other Negro poet. At times her lines are so compact that they become almost cryptic, and have to be read more than once before they will yield their meaning and beauty. Mrs. Spencer is unique in another respect; practically none of her poetry has been motivated by race. She has not been a prolific writer, and so has not yet published a collection of poems. She lives in Lynchburg, and takes great pride and pleasure in the cultivation of her beautiful garden.*

BEFORE THE FEAST OF SHUSHAN

Garden of Shushan!
After Eden, all terrace, pool, and flower recollect thee:
Ye weavers in saffron and haze and Tyrian purple,
Tell yet what range in color wakes the eye;
Sorcerer, release the dreams born here when
Drowsy, shifting palm-shade enspells the brain;
And sound! ye with harp and flute ne'er essay
Before these star-noted birds escaped from paradise awhile to

Stir all dark, and dear, and passionate desire, till mine
Arms go out to be mocked by the softly kissing body of the
    wind—
Slave, send Vashti to her King!

The fiery wattles of the sun startle into flame
The marbled towers of Shushan:
So at each day's wane, two peers—the one in
Heaven, the other on earth—welcome with their
Splendor the peerless beauty of the Queen.

Cushioned at the Queen's feet and upon her knee
Finding glory for mine head,—still, nearly shamed
Am I, the King, to bend and kiss with sharp
Breath the olive-pink of sandaled toes between;
Or lift me high to the magnet of a gaze, dusky,
Like the pool when but the moon-ray strikes to its depth;
Or closer press to crush a grape 'gainst lips redder
Than the grape, a rose in the night of her hair;
Then—Sharon's Rose in my arms.

And I am hard to force the petals wide;
And you are fast to suffer and be sad.
Is any prophet come to teach a new thing
Now in a more apt time?
Have him 'maze how you say love is sacrament;
How says Vashti, love is both bread and wine;
How to the altar may not come to break and drink,
Hulky flesh nor fleshly spirit!

I, thy lord, like not manna for meat as a Judahn;
I, thy master, drink, and red wine, plenty, and when
I thirst. Eat meat, and full, when I hunger.
I, thy King, teach you and leave you, when I list.

No woman in all Persia sets out strange action
To confuse Persia's lord—
Love is but desire and thy purpose fulfillment;
I, thy King, so say!

AT THE CARNIVAL

Gay little Girl-of-the-Diving-Tank,
I desire a name for you,
Nice, as a right glove fits;
For you—who amid the malodorous
Mechanics of this unlovely thing,
Are darling of spirit and form.
I know you—a glance, and what you are
Sits-by-the-fire in my heart.
My Limousine-Lady knows you, or
Why does the slant-envy of her eye mark
Your straight air and radiant inclusive smile?
Guilt pins a fig-leaf; Innocence is its own adorning.
The bull-necked man knows you—this first time
His itching flesh sees form divine and vibrant health
And thinks not of his avocation.
I came incuriously—
Set on no diversion save that my mind
Might safely nurse its brood of misdeeds
In the presence of a blind crowd.
The color of life was gray.
Everywhere the setting seemed right
For my mood.
Here the sausage and garlic booth
Sent unholy incense skyward;
There a quivering female-thing

Gestured assignations, and lied
To call it dancing;
There, too, were games of chance
With chances for none;
But oh! Girl-of-the-Tank, at last!
Gleaming Girl, how intimately pure and free
The gaze you send the crowd,
As though you know the dearth of beauty
In its sordid life.
We need you—my Limousine-Lady,
The bull-necked man and I.
Seeing you here brave and water-clean,
Leaven for the heavy ones of earth,
I am swift to feel that what makes
The plodder glad is good; and
Whatever is good is God.
The wonder is that you are here;
I have seen the queer in queer places,
But never before a heaven-fed
Naiad of the Carnival-Tank!
Little Diver, Destiny for you,
Like as for me, is shod in silence;
Years may seep into your soul
The bacilli of the usual and the expedient;
I implore Neptune to claim his child today!

THE WIFE-WOMAN

Maker-of-Sevens in the scheme of things
From earth to star;
Thy cycle holds whatever is fate, and
Over the border the bar.

Though rank and fierce the mariner
Sailing the seven seas,
He prays, as he holds his glass to his eyes,
Coaxing the Pleiades.

I cannot love them; and I feel your glad
Chiding from the grave,
That my all was only worth at all, what
Joy to you it gave,
These seven links the *Law* compelled
For the human chain—
I cannot love *them;* and *you,* oh,
Seven-fold months in Flanders slain!

A jungle there, a cave here, bred six
And a million years,
Sure and strong, mate for mate, such
Love as culture fears;
I gave you clear the oil and wine;
You saved me your hob and hearth—
See how *even* life may be ere the
Sickle comes and leaves a swath.

But I can wait the seven of moons,
Or years I spare,
Hoarding the heart's plenty, nor spend
A drop, nor share—
So long but outlives a smile and
A silken gown;
Then gayly I reach up from my shroud,
And you, glory-clad, reach down.

TRANSLATION

We trekked into a far country,
My friend and I.
Our deeper content was never spoken,
But each knew all the other said.
He told me how calm his soul was laid
By the lack of anvil and strife.
"The wooing kestrel," I said, "mutes his mating-note
To please the harmony of this sweet silence."
And when at the day's end
We laid tired bodies 'gainst
The loose warm sands,
And the air fleeced its particles for a coverlet;
When star after star came out
To guard their lovers in oblivion—
My soul so leapt that my evening prayer
Stole my morning song!

DUNBAR

Ah, how poets sing and die!
Make one song and Heaven takes it;
Have one heart and Beauty breaks it;
Chatterton, Shelley, Keats and I—
Ah, how poets sing and die!

COUNTEE CULLEN

COUNTEE CULLEN *was born in New York City March
30, 1903. He had a most conventional upbringing, his
home being a Methodist parsonage. He attended the city
public schools, and came out of New York University in
1925 with the degree of A.B. and a Phi Beta Kappa key.
A year later he took his A.M. at Harvard University. He
was precocious; before he had finished school in New York
he had won several important poetry prizes and gained con-
siderable reputation. In the year that he finished at New
York University, when he was but twenty-two, he published
a volume of poems that placed him at once in the list of
American poets.*

*There is not much to say about these earlier years of Cul-
len—unless he himself should say it. Quite unlike McKay or
Hughes, for example, his youth was sheltered and discloses
nothing eventful or adventurous. But all adventure is not of
the highways or high seas, of the struggle in the wilds or
in the arenas of the city. One of Cullen's earliest poems, "I
Have a Rendezvous with Life," reveals him as an adven-
turer in spirit. Even as a boy he had a lively and penetrating
curiosity about life, and this quality in him is the mainspring
of nearly all his poetry. It is the chief reason that the body of
his poetry, young as he is, constitutes a "criticism of life." It
does this more completely than the work of any other of
the major Negro poets.*

*Cullen is a fine and sensitive lyric poet, belonging to the
classic line. The modern innovators have had no influence
on him. His models are Keats and Shelley, and he might*

be called a younger brother of Housman. He never bids for popular favor through the use of bizarre effects either in manner or subject matter. He would disdain anything approaching sensationalism. All of his work is laid within the lines of the long-approved English patterns. And by that very gauge a measure of his gifts and powers as a poet may be taken. These old forms come from his hands filled with fresh beauty. A high test for a poet in this blasé age.

Some critics have ventured to state that Cullen is not an authentic Negro poet. This statement, of necessity, involves a definition of "a Negro poet" and of "Negro poetry." There might be several definitions framed, but the question raised is a pure irrelevance. Also there is in it a faint flare-up of the old taboo which would object to the use of "white" material by the Negro artist, or at least, regard it with indulgent condescension. Cullen himself has declared that, in the sense of wishing for consideration or allowances on account of race or of recognizing for himself any limitation to "racial" themes and forms, he has no desire or intention of being a Negro poet. In this he is not only within his right; he is right.

Yet, strangely, it is because Cullen revolts against these "racial" limitations—technical and spiritual—that the best of his poetry is motivated by race. He is always seeking to free himself and his art from these bonds. He never entirely escapes, but from the very fret and chafe he brings forth poetry that contains the quintessence of race-consciousness. It is through his power to deepen and heighten these inner experiences that he achieves his finest work. It is pardonable for me to repeat here that the two most poignant lines in American literature, lines that surged up from the vortex of these experiences, are in the sonnet of his in which he ex-

presses the faith that God can explain all the puzzling para-
doxes of life; then, gathering up an infinity of irony, pathos
and tragedy in the final couplet, says:

> Yet do I marvel at this curious thing—
> To make a poet black and bid him sing.

Cullen's poetry demonstrates high lyric quality, sure artis-
try, rich imagination, and intellectual content. He has, too,
the gift for witty and the power for epigrammatic expres-
sion. Pessimism is, perhaps, the pervading note in his poetry
—it is in this note that he often sings of the ephemeral qual-
ity of love—but rarely does he fail to give it a sudden ironic
turn that raises it above pathos or peevishness.
Cullen is the author of Color *(1925),* The Ballad of the
Brown Girl *(1927),* Copper Sun *(1927),* Caroling Dusk,
an anthology (1927), and The Black Christ, *containing a*
rather long narrative title poem (1929). For Color *he re-*
ceived the Harmon Gold Award for literature.

HERITAGE

> What is Africa to me:
> Copper sun or scarlet sea,
> Jungle star or jungle track,
> Strong bronzed men, or regal black
> Women from whose loins I sprang
> When the birds of Eden sang?
> *One three centuries removed*
> *From the scenes his fathers loved,*
> *Spicy grove, cinnamon tree,*
> *What is Africa to me?*

So I lie, who all day long
Want no sound except the song
Sung by wild barbaric birds
Goading massive jungle herds,
Juggernauts of flesh that pass
Trampling tall defiant grass
Where young forest lovers lie,
Plighting troth beneath the sky.
So I lie, who always hear,
Though I cram against my ear
Both my thumbs, and keep them there,
Great drums throbbing through the air.
So I lie, whose fount of pride,
Dear distress, and joy allied,
Is my somber flesh and skin,
With the dark blood dammed within
Like great pulsing tides of wine
That, I fear, must burst the fine
Channels of the chafing net
Where they surge and foam and fret.

Africa? A book one thumbs
Listlessly, till slumber comes.
Unremembered are her bats
Circling through the night, her cats
Crouching in the river reeds,
Stalking gentle flesh that feeds
By the river brink; no more
Does the bugle-throated roar
Cry that monarch claws have leapt
From the scabbards where they slept.

Silver snakes that once a year
Doff the lovely coats you wear,
Seek no covert in your fear
Lest a mortal eye should see;
What's your nakedness to me?
Here no leprous flowers rear
Fierce corollas in the air;
Here no bodies sleek and wet,
Dripping mingled rain and sweat,
Tread the savage measures of
Jungle boys and girls in love.
What is last year's snow to me,
Last year's anything? The tree
Budding yearly must forget
How its past arose or set—
Bough and blossom, flower, fruit,
Even what shy bird with mute
Wonder at her travail there,
Meekly labored in its hair.
One three centuries removed
From the scenes his fathers loved,
Spicy grove, cinnamon tree,
What is Africa to me?

So I lie, who find no peace
Night or day, no slight release
From the unremittent beat
Made by cruel padded feet
Walking through my body's street.
Up and down they go, and back,
Treading out a jungle track.

So I lie, who never quite
Safely sleep from rain at night—
I can never rest at all
When the rain begins to fall;
Like a soul gone mad with pain
I must match its weird refrain;
Ever must I twist and squirm,
Writhing like a baited worm,
While its primal measures drip
Through my body, crying, "Strip!
Doff this new exuberance.
Come and dance the Lover's Dance!"
In an old remembered way
Rain works on me night and day.

Quaint, outlandish heathen gods
Black men fashion out of rods,
Clay, and brittle bits of stone,
In a likeness like their own,
My conversion came high-priced;
I belong to Jesus Christ,
Preacher of humility;
Heathen gods are naught to me.

Father, Son, and Holy Ghost,
So I make an idle boast;
Jesus of the twice-turned cheek,
Lamb of God, although I speak
With my mouth thus, in my heart
Do I play a double part.
Ever at Thy glowing altar
Must my heart grow sick and falter,

Wishing He I served were black,
Thinking then it would not lack
Precedent of pain to guide it,
Let who would or might deride it;
Surely then this flesh would know
Yours had borne a kindred woe.
Lord, I fashion dark gods, too,
Daring even to give You
Dark despairing features where,
Crowned with dark rebellious hair,
Patience wavers just so much as
Mortal grief compels, while touches
Quick and hot, of anger, rise
To smitten cheek and weary eyes.
Lord, forgive me if my need
Sometimes shapes a human creed.

All day long and all night through,
One thing only must I do:
Quench my pride and cool my blood,
Lest I perish in the flood.
Lest a hidden ember set
Timber that I thought was wet
Burning like the dryest flax,
Melting like the merest wax,
Lest the grave restore its dead.
Not yet has my heart or head
In the least way realized
They and I are civilized.

YOUTH SINGS A SONG OF ROSEBUDS

Since men grow diffident at last,
And care no whit at all,
If spring be come, or the fall be past,
Or how the cool rains fall,

I come to no flower but I pluck,
I raise no cup but I sip,
For a mouth is the best of sweets to suck;
The oldest wine's on the lip.

If I grow old in a year or two,
And come to the querulous song
Of "Alack and aday" and "This was true,
And that, when I was young,"

I must have the sweets to remember by,
Some blossom saved from the mire,
Some death-rebellious ember I
Can fan into a fire.

TO JOHN KEATS, POET, AT SPRINGTIME

I cannot hold my peace, John Keats;
There never was a spring like this;
It is an echo, that repeats
My last year's song and next year's bliss.
I know, in spite of all men say
Of Beauty, you have felt her most.
Yea, even in your grave her way
Is laid. Poor, troubled, lyric ghost,

Spring never was so fair and dear
As Beauty makes her seem this year.

I cannot hold my peace, John Keats,
I am as helpless in the toil
Of Spring as any lamb that bleats
To feel the solid earth recoil
Beneath his puny legs. Spring beats
Her tocsin call to those who love her,
And lo! the dogwood petals cover
Her breast with drifts of snow, and sleek
White gulls fly screaming to her, and hover
About her shoulders, and kiss her cheek,
While white and purple lilacs muster
A strength that bears them to a cluster
Of color and odor; for her sake
All things that slept are now awake.

And you and I, shall we lie still,
John Keats, while Beauty summons us?
Somehow I feel your sensitive will
Is pulsing up some tremulous
Sap road of a maple tree, whose leaves
Grow music as they grow, since your
Wild voice is in them, a harp that grieves
For life that opens death's dark door.
Though dust, your fingers still can push
The Vision Splendid to a birth,
Though now they work as grass in the hush
Of the night on the broad sweet page of the earth.

"John Keats is dead," they say, but I
Who hear your full insistent cry

In bud and blossom, leaf and tree,
Know John Keats still writes poetry.
And while my head is earthward bowed
To read new life sprung from your shroud,
Folks seeing me must think it strange
That merely spring should so derange
My mind. They do not know that you,
John Keats, keep revel with me, too.

FROM THE DARK TOWER

We shall not always plant while others reap
The golden increment of bursting fruit,
Not always countenance, abject and mute,
That lesser men should hold their brothers cheap;
Not everlastingly while others sleep
Shall we beguile their limbs with mellow flute,
Not always bend to some more subtle brute;
We were not made eternally to weep.

The night whose sable breast relieves the stark,
White stars is no less lovely being dark,
And there are buds that cannot bloom at all
In light, but crumple, piteous, and fall;
So in the dark we hide the heart that bleeds,
And wait, and tend our agonizing seeds.

TIMID LOVER

I who employ a poet's tongue,
Would tell you how
You are a golden damson hung
Upon a silver bough.

I who adore exotic things
Would shape a sound
To be your name, a word that sings
Until the head goes round.

I who am proud with other folk
Would grow complete
In pride on bitter words you spoke,
And kiss your petaled feet.

But never past the frail intent
My will may flow,
Though gentle looks of yours are bent
Upon me where I go.

So must I, starved for love's delight,
Affect the mute,
When love's divinest acolyte
Extends me holy fruit.

UNCLE JIM

"White folks is white," says Uncle Jim;
"A platitude," I sneer;
And then I tell him so is milk,
And the froth upon his beer.

His heart walled up with bitterness,
He smokes his pungent pipe,
And nods at me as if to say,
"Young fool, you'll soon be ripe!"

I have a friend who eats his heart
Away with grief of mine,
Who drinks my joy as tipplers drain
Deep goblets filled with wine.

I wonder why here at his side,
Face-in-the-grass with him,
My mind should stray the Grecian urn
To muse on Uncle Jim.

BLACK MAGDALENS

These have no Christ to spit and stoop
    To write upon the sand,
Inviting him that has not sinned
    To raise the first rude hand.

And if he came they could not buy
    Rich ointment for his feet,
The body's sale scarce yields enough
    To let the body eat.

The chaste clean ladies pass them by
    And draw their skirts aside,
But Magdalens have a ready laugh;
    They wrap their wounds in pride.

They fare full ill since Christ forsook
    The cross to mount a throne,
And Virtue still is stooping down
    To cast the first hard stone.

TABLEAU

Locked arm in arm they cross the way,
   The black boy and the white,
The golden splendor of the day,
   The sable pride of night.

From lowered blinds the dark folk stare,
   And here the fair folk talk,
Indignant that these two should dare
   In unison to walk.

Oblivious to look and word
   They pass, and see no wonder
That lightning brilliant as a sword
   Should blaze the path of thunder.

YET DO I MARVEL

I doubt not God is good, well-meaning, kind,
And did He stoop to quibble could tell why
The little buried mole continues blind,
Why flesh that mirrors Him must some day die,
Make plain the reason tortured Tantalus
Is baited by the fickle fruit, declare
If merely brute caprice dooms Sisyphus
To struggle up a never-ending stair.
Inscrutable His ways are, and immune
To catechism by a mind too strewn
With petty cares to slightly understand
What awful brain compels His awful hand.
Yet do I marvel at this curious thing:
To make a poet black, and bid him sing!

LANGSTON HUGHES

LANGSTON HUGHES *was born in Joplin, Mo., February 1, 1902, the son of educated parents; his father was a lawyer and his mother a school teacher. A part of his boyhood he spent with his maternal grandmother at Lawrence, Kansas. This grandmother was first married to Lewis Sheridan Leary, one of the five Negroes with John Brown at Harper's Ferry, and one of the men killed during the raid. She afterward married Charles Langston, the grandfather of Langston Hughes. Charles was the brother of John M. Langston, the famous Negro orator, and at one time a member of Congress representing the State of Virginia.*

Hughes attended the public schools of Lawrence. In his fourteenth year he moved with his mother to Cleveland, Ohio, where he was graduated from high school. In his senior year he was elected class poet. He next went to Mexico City and spent more than a year with his father, who had been located there for some time. He came to New York in 1921 and entered Columbia University. After a year there he had a break with his father and started out to earn his living. He worked first on a Staten Island truck farm; next he was a delivery boy for a New York florist; then he signed on as a member of the crew of a freight steamer and for two years voyaged to the Canary Islands, the Azores, and the West Coast of Africa. On his twenty-second birthday he shipped from New York for Europe. Three weeks later he found himself in Paris, practically broke. He got a job as doorman at a Montmartre cabaret. Later he became second cook at the Grand Duc, a Negro night club. Toward the end of the summer he went to Italy, and September found him stranded in Genoa. He worked his way back home on a tramp steamer, painting and scrubbing decks, reaching New York in November, 1924. Out of these varied experiences he wrote a number of poems.

On his return Hughes went to Washington, where he stayed a year, working in the offices of Dr. Carter G. Woodson, editor of the Journal of Negro History, and afterward as a bus boy at the Wardman Park Hotel. In this latter capacity he came into touch with Vachel Lindsay, who read some of his poems, and this led to the discovery of Hughes by the newspapers. In the following year his first volume, The Weary Blues, appeared. He then determined to resume his formal education. He entered Lincoln University and was graduated in 1929. In 1925 he won the first prize for poetry in the Opportunity contest, and in 1926, while he was a student at Lincoln, he was awarded the Witter Bynner undergraduate poetry prize.

It is natural, indeed inevitable, to juxtapose Hughes and Cullen. A comparison shows them to be of about the same age and winning national recognition at almost the same time. But the contrast is more striking. Hughes began to buffet the world in his 'teens. Before he was twenty-one he had experienced varied and harsh phases of life. The contrast between the work of the two young poets is as great as the contrast between the days of their youth. Hughes is a cosmopolite and a rebel, and both of these attributes are reflected in his poetry. As a rebel, he will not be bound by poetic form and traditions. As a cosmopolite, he takes his subject matter from any level of life that interests him. His forms are for the most part free, and his subject matter is often from the lower strata. Also, Hughes is the more objective. He is more apt than Cullen to portray life as he sees it *rather than as he feels it. He is possessed of a sardonic quality that enables him to give the cynical twist that is seen in "Mulatto," "Cross," and other poems. Through this same quality he often lifts a poem clear above the level of its origin. This is well illustrated in the last ten lines of "Brass Spittoons." Consciously, race means very little to Hughes; nevertheless, like Cullen, he is largely motivated by it in his work, and cannot altogether escape it. From it he, too, achieves his finest and most vivid effects.*

A great deal of Hughes's poetry is written in the Negro folk and jazz rhythms, the fundamental rhythms in which Vachel Lindsay experimented when he wrote "The Congo," "Simon Legree," "John Brown," and "General William Booth Enters Heaven." But Hughes has developed and perfected an individual technique. There are poems, too—for example, "The Negro Speaks of Rivers"—in which he shows himself a superb lyrist.

He published The Weary Blues *in 1926,* Fine Clothes to the Jew *in 1927, and* Not Without Laughter, *a novel, in 1930, which won the Harmon Gold Award.*

BRASS SPITTOONS

Clean the spittoons, boy.
    Detroit,
    Chicago,
    Atlantic City,
    Palm Beach.
Clean the spittoons.
The steam in hotel kitchens,
And the smoke in hotel lobbies,
And the slime in hotel spittoons:

Part of my life.
　　　Hey, boy!
　　　A nickel,
　　　A dime,
　　　A dollar,
Two dollars a day.
　　　Hey, boy!
　　　A nickel,
　　　A dime,
　　　A dollar,
　　　Two dollars
Buys shoes for the baby.
House rent to pay.
Gin on Saturday,
Church on Sunday.
　　　My God!
Babies and gin and church
and women and Sunday
all mixed with dimes and
dollars and clean spittoons
and house rent to pay.
　　　Hey, boy!
A bright bowl of brass is beautiful to the Lord.
Bright polished brass like the cymbals
Of King David's dancers,
Like the wine cups of Solomon.
　　　Hey, boy!
A clean spittoon on the altar of the Lord.
A clean bright spittoon all newly polished—
At least I can offer that.
　　　Com'mere, boy!

JAZZONIA

Oh, silver tree!
Oh, shining rivers of the soul!

In a Harlem cabaret
Six long-headed jazzers play.
A dancing girl whose eyes are bold
Lifts high a dress of silken gold.

Oh, singing tree!
Oh, shining rivers of the soul!

Were Eve's eyes
In the first garden
Just a bit too bold?
Was Cleopatra gorgeous
In a gown of gold?

Oh, shining tree!
Oh, silver rivers of the soul!

In a whirling cabaret
Six long-headed jazzers play.

CROSS

My old man's a white old man
And my old mother's black.
If ever I cursed my white old man
I take my curses back.

If ever I cursed my black old mother
And wished she were in hell,
I'm sorry for that evil wish
And now I wish her well.

My old man died in a fine big house.
My ma died in a shack.
I wonder where I'm gonna die,
Being neither white nor black?

PO' BOY BLUES

When I was home de
Sunshine seemed like gold.
When I was home de
Sunshine seemed like gold.
Since I come up North de
Whole damn world's turned cold.

I was a good boy,
Never done no wrong.
Yes, I was a good boy,
Never done no wrong,
But this world is weary
An' de road is hard an' long.

I fell in love with
A gal I thought was kind.
Fell in love with
A gal I thought was kind.
She made me lose ma money
An' almost lose ma mind.

Weary, weary,
Weary early in de morn.
Weary, weary,
Early, early in de morn.
I's so weary
I wish I'd never been born.

HARD DADDY

I went to ma daddy,
Says Daddy I have got de blues.
Went to ma daddy,
Says Daddy I have got de blues.
Ma daddy says, Honey,
Can't you bring no better news?

I cried on his shoulder but
He turned his back on me.
Cried on his shoulder but
He turned his back on me.
He said a woman's cryin's
Never gonna bother me.

I wish I had wings to
Fly like de eagle flies.
Wish I had wings to
Fly like de eagle flies.
I'd fly on ma man an'
I'd scratch out both his eyes.

ESTHETE IN HARLEM

Strange,
That in this nigger place
I should meet life face to face;
When, for years, I had been seeking
Life in places gentler-speaking,
Until I came to this vile street
And found Life stepping on my feet!

JAZZ BAND IN A PARISIAN CABARET

Play that thing,
Jazz band!
Play it for the lords and ladies,
For the dukes and counts,
For the whores and gigolos,
For the American millionaires,
And the school teachers
Out for a spree.
Play it,
Jazz band!
You know that tune
That laughs and cries at the same time.
You know it.

> May I?
> Mais oui.
> Mein Gott!
> Parece una rumba.

Play it, jazz band!
You've got seven languages to speak in

And then some,
"Even if you do come from Georgia,
        Can I go home wid yuh, sweetie?"
        "Sure."

AS I GREW OLDER

It was a long time ago.
I have almost forgotten my dream.
But it was there then,
In front of me,
Bright like a sun—
My dream.

And then the wall rose,
Rose slowly,
Slowly,
Between me and my dream.
Rose slowly, slowly,
Dimming,
Hiding,
The light of my dream.
Rose until it touched the sky—
The wall.

Shadow.
I am black.

I lie down in the shadow.
No longer the light of my dream before me,
Above me.
Only the thick wall.
Only the shadow.

My hands!
My dark hands!
Break through the wall!
Find my dream!
Help me to shatter this darkness,
To smash this night,
To break this shadow
Into a thousand lights of sun,
Into a thousand whirling dreams
Of sun!

THE NEGRO SPEAKS OF RIVERS

I've known rivers:
I've known rivers ancient as the world and older than the
   flow of human blood in human veins.

My soul has grown deep like the rivers.

I bathed in the Euphrates when dawns were young.
I built my hut near the Congo and it lulled me to sleep.
I looked upon the Nile and raised the pyramids above it.
I heard the singing of the Mississippi when Abe Lincoln
   went down to New Orleans, and I've seen its muddy
   bosom turn all golden in the sunset.

I've known rivers:
Ancient, dusky rivers.

My soul has grown deep like rivers.

FANTASY IN PURPLE

Beat the drums of tragedy for me.
Beat the drums of tragedy and death.
And let the choir sing a stormy song
To drown the rattle of my dying breath.

Beat the drums of tragedy for me,
And let the white violins whir thin and slow,
But blow one blaring trumpet note of sun
To go with me
                        to the darkness
                                    where I go.

GWENDOLYN BENNETT

G WENDOLYN BENNETT *was born in Giddings, Texas, July 8, 1902. Her father was a lawyer and her mother a school teacher. She received her elementary education in the public schools of Washington and was graduated in 1921 from the Girls' High School in Brooklyn, New York. Miss Bennett is both an artist and a poet. She studied in the Fine Arts Department of Teachers College, Columbia University, for two years, and in 1924 she was graduated from Pratt Institute, Brooklyn. After finishing at Pratt she was engaged as instructor in water-color and design in the Fine Arts Department of Howard University. Shortly afterward she was awarded the Thousand Dollar Foreign Scholarship of the Delta Sigma Theta Sorority. She went to Europe in the summer of 1925 and studied for a year in Paris at the Académie Julian and the École de Panthéon. On her return she became for a while a member of the editorial staff of* Opportunity. *Miss Bennett is the author of a number of fine poems, some of them in the freer forms, but she is her best in the delicate, poignant lyrics that she has written.*

TO A DARK GIRL

I love you for your brownness
And the rounded darkness of your breast.
I love you for the breaking sadness in your voice
And shadows where your wayward eye-lids rest.

Something of old forgotten queens
Lurks in the lithe abandon of your walk,
And something of the shackled slave
Sobs in the rhythm of your talk.

Oh, little brown girl, born for sorrow's mate,
Keep all you have of queenliness,
Forgetting that you once were slave,
And let your full lips laugh at Fate!

NOCTURNE

This cool night is strange
Among midsummer days . . .
Far frosts are caught
In the moon's pale light,
And sounds are distant laughter
Chilled to crystal tears.

SONNET—2

Some things are very dear to me—
Such things as flowers bathed by rain
Or patterns traced upon the sea
Or crocuses where snow has lain . . .
The iridescence of a gem,
The moon's cool opalescent light,
Azaleas and the scent of them,
And honeysuckles in the night.
And many sounds are also dear—
Like winds that sing among the trees
Or crickets calling from the weir

Or Negroes humming melodies.
But dearer far than all surmise
Are sudden tear-drops in your eyes.

HERITAGE

I want to see the slim palm-trees,
Pulling at the clouds
With little pointed fingers. . . .

I want to see lithe Negro girls,
Etched dark against the sky
While sunset lingers.

I want to hear the silent sands,
Singing to the moon
Before the Sphinx-still face. . . .

I want to hear the chanting
Around a heathen fire
Of a strange black race.

I want to breathe the Lotus flow'r,
Sighing to the stars
With tendrils drinking at the Nile. . . .

I want to feel the surging
Of my sad people's soul
Hidden by a minstrel-smile.

HATRED

I shall hate you
Like a dart of singing steel
Shot through still air
At even-tide.
Or solemnly
As pines are sober
When they stand etched
Against the sky.
Hating you shall be a game
Played with cool hands
And slim fingers.
Your heart will yearn
For the lonely splendor
Of the pine tree;
While rekindled fires
In my eyes
Shall wound you like swift arrows.
Memory will lay its hands
Upon your breast
And you will understand
My hatred.

STERLING A. BROWN

STERLING A. BROWN *was born in Washington, D.C., May 1, 1901. He received his primary and secondary education in the public schools of that city. In 1918 he entered Williams College, and in his junior year was elected to Phi Beta Kappa. He was graduated in 1922 and in the following year received his A.M. at Harvard University. He has taught school in several institutions and is now professor of English at Howard University.*

He is one of the outstanding poets of the younger group. For the best of his work he has dug his raw material from the great mine of Negro folk poetry. More than any other American poet he has made thematic use of the Negro folk epics and ballads, and because he has done this so sincerely, a false note is rarely heard in his work. He has not made mere transcriptions of this folk poetry, and he has done much more than bring to it mere artistry; he has deepened its meanings and multiplied its implications. He has developed a unique technique, one that does not depend primarily upon rhythmic imitation. He has really absorbed the spirit of this poetry, made it his own, and, without diluting its primitive frankness and raciness, truly reëxpressed it with artistry and magnified power. He has perceived that one of the cardinal traits of Negro folk poetry is terseness—a trait at complete variance with the general idea of Negro diffuseness—and strictly adhered to it. He has, in fact, done the only thing that justifies the individual artist in taking material of this sort: he has worked it into original and genuine poetry.

Sterling A. Brown has not confined himself exclusively to poetry written on these themes; he is also the author of a number of fine poems of a universal character done in literary English.

ODYSSEY OF BIG BOY

Lemme be wid Casey Jones,
   Lemme be wid Stagolee,
Lemme be wid such like men
   When Death takes hol' on me,
     When Death takes hol' on me. . . .

Done skinned as a boy in Kentucky hills,
   Druv steel dere as a man,
Done stripped tobacco in Virginia fiel's
   Alongst de River Dan,
     Alongst de River Dan;

Done mined de coal in West Virginia
   Liked dat job jes' fine
Till a load o' slate curved roun' my head
   Won't work in no mo' mine,
     Won't work in no mo' mine;

Done shocked de corn in Marylan',
   In Georgia done cut cane,
Done planted rice in South Caline,
   But won't do dat again
     Do dat no mo' again.

Been roustabout in Memphis,
   Dockhand in Baltimore,

Done smashed up freight on Norfolk wharves
A fust class stevedore,
A fust class stevedore. . . .

Done slung hash yonder in de North
On de ole Fall River Line
Done busted suds in li'l New Yawk
Which ain't no work o' mine—
Lawd, ain't no work o' mine.

Done worked and loafed on such like jobs
Seen what dey is to see
Done had my time with a pint on my hip
An' a sweet gal on my knee
Sweet mommer on my knee:

Had stovepipe blonde in Macon
Yaller gal in Marylan'
In Richmond had a choklit brown
Called me huh monkey man—
Huh big fool monkey man.

Had two fair browns in Arkansaw
And three in Tennessee
Had Creole gal in New Orleans
Sho Gawd did two time me—
Lawd two time, fo' time me—

But best gal what I evah had
Done put it over dem
A gal in Southwest Washington
At Four'n half and M—
Four'n half and M. . . .

Done took my livin' as it came
   Done grabbed my joy, done risked my life
Train done caught me on de trestle
   Man done caught me wid his wife
      His doggone purty wife. . . .

I done had my women,
   I done had my fun
Cain't do much complainin'
   When my jag is done,
      Lawd, Lawd, my jag is done.

An' all dat Big Boy axes
   When time comes fo' to go
Lemme be wid John Henry, steel drivin' man
   Lemme be wid ole Jazzbo;
      Lemme be wid ole Jazzbo. . . .

SOUTHERN ROAD

Swing dat hammer—hunh—
Steady, bo.
Swing dat hammer—hunh—
Steady, bo;
Ain't no rush, bebby,
Long ways to go.

Burner tore his—hunh—
Black heart away;
Burner tore his—hunh—
Black heart away;
Got me life, bebby,
An' a day.

Gal's on Fifth Street—hunh—
Son done gone;
Gal's on Fifth Street—hunh—
Son done gone;
Wife's in de ward, bebby,
Babe's not bo'n.

My ole man died—hunh—
Cussin' me;
My ole man died—hunh—
Cussin' me;
Ole lady rocks, bebby,
Huh misery.

Doubleshackled—hunh—
Guard behin';
Doubleshackled—hunh—
Guard behin';
Ball an' chain, bebby,
On my min'.

White man tells me—hunh—
Damn yo' soul;
White man tells me—hunh—
Damn yo' soul;
Got no need, bebby,
To be tole.

Chain gang nevah—hunh—
Let me go;
Chain gang nevah—hunh—
Let me go;
Po' los' boy, bebby,
Evahmo' . . .

MEMPHIS BLUES

1

Nineveh, Tyre
Babylon,
Not much lef'
Of either one.
All dese cities
Ashes and rust,
De win' sing sperrichals
Through deir dus'. . . .
Was another Memphis
Mongst de olden days,
Done been destroyed
In many ways. . . .
Dis here Memphis
It may go
Floods may drown it;
Tornado blow;
Mississippi wash it
Down to sea—
Like de other Memphis in
History.

2

Watcha gonna do when Memphis on fire,
  Memphis on fire, Mistah Preachin' Man?
Gonna pray to Jesus and nebber tire,
  Gonna pray to Jesus, loud as I can,
    Gonna pray to my Jesus, oh, my Lawd!

Watcha gonna do when de tall flames roar,
  Tall flames roar, Mistah Lovin' Man?
Gonna love my brownskin better'n before—
  Gonna love my baby lak a do right man,
    Gonna love my brown baby, oh, my Lawd!

Watcha gonna do when Memphis falls down,
  Memphis falls down, Mistah Music Man?
Gonna plunk on dat box as long as it soun',
  Gonna plunk dat box fo' to beat de ban',
    Gonna tickle dem ivories, oh, my Lawd!

Watcha gonna do in de hurricane,
  In de hurricane, Mistah Workin' Man?
Gonna put dem buildings up again,
  Gonna put em up dis time to stan',
    Gonna push a wicked wheelbarrow, oh, my Lawd!

Watcha gonna do when Memphis near gone,
  Memphis near gone, Mistah Drinkin' Man?
Gonna grab a pint bottle of Mountain Corn,
  Gonna keep de stopper in my han',
    Gonna get a mean jag on, oh, my Lawd!

Watcha gonna do when de flood roll fas',
  Flood roll fas', Mistah Gamblin' Man?
Gonna pick up my dice fo' one las' pass—
  Gonna fade my way to de lucky lan',
    Gonna throw my las' seven—oh, my Lawd!

3

Memphis go
By Flood or Flame;

Nigger won't worry
All de same—
Memphis go
Memphis come back,
Ain' no skin
Off de nigger's back.
All dese cities
Ashes, rust. . . .
De win' sing sperrichals
Through deir dus'.

LONG GONE

I laks yo' kin' of lovin'
    Ain't never caught you wrong
But it jes ain' nachal
    Fo' to stay here long;

It jes ain' nachal
    Fo' a railroad man
With a itch fo' travelin'
    He cain't understan'. . . .

I looks at de rails
    An' I looks at de ties
An' I hears an ole freight
    Puffin' up de rise,

An' at nights on my pallet
    When all is still
I listens fo' de empties
    Bumpin' up de hill;

When I oughta be quiet
   I is got a itch
Fo' to hear de whistle blow
   Fo' de crossin' or de switch.

An' I knows de time's a nearin'
   When I got to ride
Though it's homelike and happy
   At your side.

You is done all you could do
   To make me stay;
'Tain't no fault of yours I'se leavin'—
   I'se jes dataway.

I is got to see some people
   I ain' never seen,
Gotta highball thu some country
   Whah I never been. . . .

I don't know which way I'm travelin'—
   Far or near,
All I knows fo' certain is
   I cain't stay here.

Ain't no call at all, sweet woman,
   Fo' to carry on—
Jes my name and jes my habit
   To be Long Gone. . . .

SLIM GREER

Listen to the tale
Of Ole Slim Greer,
Waitines' devil
Waitin' here;

Talkines' guy,
An' biggest liar,
With always a new lie
On the fire.

Tells a tale
Of Arkansaw
That keeps the kitchen
In a roar;

Tells in a long-drawled
Careless tone,
As solemn as a Baptist
Parson's moan;

How he in Arkansaw
Passed for white
An' he no lighter
Than a dark midnight.

Found a nice white woman
At a dance,
Thought he was from Spain
Or else from France;

Nobody suspicioned
Old Slim Greer's race
But a Hill Billy, always
Roun' the place,

> Who called one day
> On the trustful dame
> An' found Slim comfy
> When he came.

The whites lef' the parlor
All to Slim,
Which didn't cut
No ice with him,

> An' he started a tinklin'
> Some mo'nful blues,
> An' a-pattin' the time
> With No. Fourteen shoes.

The cracker listened
An' then he spat
An' said, "No white man
Could play like that. . . ."

> The white jane ordered
> The tattler out;
> Then, female-like,
> Began to doubt,

Crept into the parlor
Soft as you please,
Where Slim was agitatin'
The ivories.

Heard Slim's music—
An' then, hot damn!
Shouted sharp—"Nigger!"
An' Slim said, "Ma'am?"

She screamed and the crackers
Swarmed up soon,
But found only echoes
Of his tune;

'Cause Slim had sold out
With lightnin' speed;
"Hope I may die, sir—
Yes, indeed. . . ."

STRONG MEN

They dragged you from homeland,
They chained you in coffles,
They huddled you spoon-fashion in filthy hatches,
They sold you to give a few gentlemen ease.

They broke you in like oxen,
They scourged you,
They branded you,
They made your women breeders,
They swelled your numbers with bastards. . . .
They taught you the religion they disgraced.

You sang:
    Keep a inchin' along
    Lak a po' inch worm. . . .

You sang:
>   *Bye and bye*
>   *I'm gonna lay down dis heaby load. . . .*

You sang.
>   *Walk togedder, chillen,*
>   *Dontcha git weary. . . .*
>   The strong men keep a-comin' on
>   The strong men git stronger.

They point with pride to the roads you built for them,
They ride in comfort over the rails you laid for them.
They put hammers in your hands
And said—Drive so much before sundown.

You sang:
>   *Ain't no hammah*
>   *In dis lan',*
>   *Strikes lak mine, bebby,*
>   *Strikes lak mine.*

They cooped you in their kitchens,
They penned you in their factories,
They gave you the jobs that they were too good for,
They tried to guarantee happiness to themselves
By shunting dirt and misery to you.

You sang:
>   *Me an' muh baby gonna shine, shine*
>   *Me an' muh baby gonna shine.*
>   The strong men keep a-comin' on
>   The strong men git stronger . . .

They bought off some of your leaders
You stumbled, as blind men will . . .
They coaxed you, unwontedly soft voiced . . .
You followed a way.
Then laughed as usual.
They heard the laugh and wondered;
Uncomfortable;
Unadmitting a deeper terror. . . .
> The strong men keep a-comin' on
> Gittin' stronger. . . .

What, from the slums
Where they have hemmed you,
What, from the tiny huts
They could not keep from you—
What reaches them
Making them ill at ease, fearful?
Today they shout prohibition at you
"Thou shalt not this"
"Thou shalt not that"
"Reserved for whites only"
You laugh.

One thing they cannot prohibit—
> The strong men . . . coming on
> The strong men gittin' stronger.
> Strong men . . .
> Stronger . . .

EFFIE

She who was easy for any chance lover,
Whose frequent laugh rang flaccid and shrill;
She, finding death at last, the dazed fret over,
Lies here so oddly stern for once, and still.

Put her away, and put away with her
What she has now of harshness and strength,
She who was clay for any clumsy sculptor
Becomes inflexible; fixed of form at length.

She who would veer with any passing wind
Like a rusty vane with rickety ways,
She is aloof now, and seems—oh, so determined;
And that is the Paradise crowning her days.

ARNA BONTEMPS

Arna Bontemps *was born in Alexandria, Louisiana,*
1902. He attended the public schools of Los Angeles
and high school at San Fernando, Cal. He was for a while a
student of the University of California (Southern). In 1923
he was graduated with honors from Pacific Union.

Like Countee Cullen, Arna Bontemps works in literary
English and in the standard forms. He has, however, experi-
mented in free verse; in his "Golgotha Is a Mountain" the
experiment is markedly successful. He is calm and contem-
plative, and writes in a quiet, even tone. His fire does not
flash or flame but burns with a steady glow. His work shows
skill and constant care; and while it never rises to heights
of passion and ecstasy, neither does it ever fall to bathos or
slipshod workmanship. He is the author of a novel, God
Sends Sunday.

He now lives in New York, and is a teacher in a private
school.

A BLACK MAN TALKS OF REAPING

I have sown beside all waters in my day.
I planted deep within my heart the fear
'That wind or fowl would take the grain away.
I planted safe against this stark, lean year.

I scattered seed enough to plant the land
In rows from Canada to Mexico.
But for my reaping only what the hand
Can hold at once is all that I can show.

Yet what I sowed and what the orchard yields
My brother's sons are gathering stalk and root,
Small wonder then my children glean in fields
They have not sown, and feed on bitter fruit.

SOUTHERN MANSION

Poplars are standing there still as death
And ghosts of dead men
Meet their ladies walking
Two by two beneath the shade
And standing on the marble steps.

There is a sound of music echoing
Through the open door
And in the field there is
Another sound tinkling in the cotton:
Chains of bondmen dragging on the ground

The years go back with an iron clank,
A hand is on the gate,
A dry leaf trembles on the wall.
Ghosts are walking.
They have broken roses down
And poplars stand there still as death.

NOCTURNE OF THE WHARVES

All night they whine upon their ropes and boom
Against the dock with helpless prows:
These little ships that are too worn for sailing
From the wharf but do not rest at all.

Tugging at the dim gray wharf they think
No doubt of China and of bright Bombay.
And they remember islands of the East,
Formosa and the mountains of Japan.
They think of cities ruined by the sea
And they are restless, sleeping at the wharf.

Tugging at the dim gray wharf they think
No less of Africa. An east wind blows
And salt spray sweeps the unattended decks.
Shouts of dead men break upon the night.
The captain calls his crew and they respond—
The little ships are dreaming—land is near.
But mist comes up to dim the copper coast,
Mist dissembles images of the trees.
The captain and his men alike are lost
And their shouts go down in the rising sound of waves.

Ah little ships, I know your weariness!
I know the sea-green shadows of your dream.
For I have loved the cities of the sea
And desolations of the old days I
Have loved: I was a wanderer like you
And I have broken down before the wind.

BLIGHT

I have seen a lovely thing
Stark before a whip of weather:
The tree that was so wistful after spring
Beating barren twigs together.

The birds that came there one by one,
The sensuous leaves that used to sway
And whisper there at night, all are gone,
Each has vanished in its way.

And this whip is on my heart;
There is no sound that it allows,
No little song that I may start
But I hear the beating of dead boughs.

NOCTURNE AT BETHESDA

I thought I saw an angel flying low,
I thought I saw the flicker of a wing
Above the mulberry trees; but not again.
Bethesda sleeps. This ancient pool that healed
A host of bearded Jews does not awake.
This pool that once the angels troubled does not move.
No angel stirs it now, no Saviour comes
With healing in His hands to raise the sick
And bid the lame man leap upon the ground.

The golden days are gone. Why do we wait
So long upon the marble steps, blood
Falling from our open wounds? and why
Do our black faces search the empty sky?
Is there something we have forgotten? some precious thing
We have lost, wandering in strange lands?

There was a day, I remember now,
I beat my breast and cried, "Wash me, God,
Wash me with a wave of wind upon

The barley; O quiet One, draw near, draw near!
Walk upon the hills with lovely feet
And in the waterfall stand and speak.

"Dip white hands in the lily pool and mourn
Upon the harps still hanging in the trees
Near Babylon along the river's edge,
But oh, remember me, I pray, before
The summer goes and rose leaves lose their red."

The old terror takes my heart, the fear
Of quiet waters and of faint twilights.
There will be better days when I am gone
And healing pools where I cannot be healed.
Fragrant stars will gleam forever and ever
Above the place where I lie desolate.

Yet I hope, still I long to live.
And if there can be returning after death
I shall come back. But it will not be here;
If you want me you must search for me
Beneath the palms of Africa. Or if
I am not there then you may call to me
Across the shining dunes, perhaps I shall
Be following a desert caravan.

I may pass through centuries of death
With quiet eyes, but I'll remember still
A jungle tree with burning scarlet birds.
There is something I have forgotten, some precious thing.
I shall be seeking ornaments of ivory,
I shall be dying for a jungle fruit.

You do not hear, Bethesda.
O still green water in a stagnant pool!
Love abandoned you and me alike.
There was a day you held a rich full moon
Upon your heart and listened to the words
Of men now dead and saw the angels fly.
There is a simple story on your face;
Years have wrinkled you. I know, Bethesda!
You are sad. It is the same with me.

GOD GIVE TO MEN

God give the yellow man
An easy breeze at blossom time.
Grant his eager, slanting eyes to cover
Every land and dream
Of afterwhile.

Give blue-eyed men their swivel chairs
To whirl in tall buildings.
Allow them many ships at sea,
And on land, soldiers
And policemen.

For black man, God,
No need to bother more
But only fill afresh his meed
Of laughter,
His cup of tears.

God suffer little men
The taste of soul's desire.

FRANK HORNE

FRANK HORNE *was born in New York City, August 18, 1899. After finishing the public schools he entered the College of the City of New York, where he won his varsity letters on the track team and wrote his first poem. Later he attended the Northern Illinois College of Ophthalmology and was graduated with the degree of Doctor of Optometry. He practiced for a while in Chicago and in New York. He is at present a member of the faculty of the Fort Valley High and Industrial School at Fort Valley, Georgia. It is his ambition to be a prose writer, but notwithstanding, he is one of the best known of the younger group of poets. His "Letters Found Near a Suicide" was the prize poem in the* Crisis *contest, 1925. He is in every sense modern. He uses the freer forms and strips phraseology down to the firm, essential framework. He never pads the idea or the line with poetical prettyisms, and in his work there is an entire absence of smooth-worn clichés. As a result, his effects are clear and sharp. In a number of his poems he reveals a philosophical strain; that is, he takes life and its meanings into consideration. But he does this in no contemplative or optimistic mood. He is ironical and skeptical, and his philosophy is often gathered up into a keen thrust. He possesses the authentic gift of poetry.*

NIGGER

A Chant for Children

Little Black boy
Chased down the street—

"Nigger, nigger never die
Black face an' shiny eye,
Nigger . . . nigger . . . nigger . . ."

Hannibal . . . Hannibal
Bangin' through the Alps
Licked the proud Romans,
Ran home with their scalps—
"Nigger . . . nigger . . . nigger . . ."

Othello . . . black man
Mighty in war
Listened to Iago,
Called his wife a whore—
"Nigger . . . nigger . . . nigger . . ."

Crispus . . . Attucks
Bullets in his chest
Red blood of freedom
Runnin' down his vest
"Nigger . . . nigger . . . nigger . . ."

Toussaint . . . Toussaint
Made the French flee
Fought like a demon
Set his people free—
"Nigger . . . nigger . . . nigger . . ."

Jesus . . . Jesus
Son of the Lord
—Spit in his face
—Nail him on a board
"Nigger . . . nigger . . . nigger . . ."

Little Black boy
Runs down the street—
"Nigger, nigger never die
Black face an' shiny eye,
Nigger . . . nigger . . ."

MORE LETTERS FOUND NEAR A SUICIDE

To the Poets:
Why do poets
Like to die
And sing raptures to the grave?

They seem to think
That bitter dirt
Turns sweet between the teeth.

I have lived
And yelled hosannas
At the climbing stars

I have lived
And drunk deep
The deceptive wine of life. . . .

And now, tipsy and reeling
From its dregs
I die . . .

Oh, let the poets sing
Raptures to the grave.

To Henry:

    I do not know
    How I shall look
    When I lie down here
    But I really should be smiling
    Mischievously . . .
    You and I have studied
    Together
    The knowledge of the ages
    And lived the life of Science
    Matching discovery for discovery—
    And yet
    In a trice
    With a small explosion
    Of this little machine
    In my hand
    I shall know
    All
    That Aristotle, Newton, Lavoisier, and Galileo
    Could not determine
    In their entire
    Lifetimes . . .
    And the joke of it is,
    Henry,
    That I have
    Beat you to it . . .

To One Who Called Me "Nigger":

    You are Power
    And send steel ships hurtling
    From shore to shore . . .

You are Vision
And cast your sight through eons of space
From world to world . . .

You are Brain
And throw your voice endlessly
From ear to ear . . .

You are Soul
And falter at the yawning chasm
From White to Black . . .

To Caroline:
Your piano
Is the better instrument . .
Yesterday
Your fingers
So precisely
Touched the cold keys—
A nice string
Of orderly sounds
A proper melody . . .
Tonight
Your hands
So wantonly
Caressed my tingling skin—
A mad whirl
Of cacophony,
A wild chanting . . .
Your piano
Is the better instrument.

To Alfred:
I have grown tired of you
And your wife
Sitting there
With your children,
Little bits of you
Running about your feet
And you two so calm
And cold together . . .
It is really better
To lie here
Insensate
Than to see new life
Creep upon you
Calm and cold
Sitting there . . .

To You:
All my life
They have told me
That You
Would save my Soul
That only
By kneeling in Your House
And eating of Your Body
And drinking of Your Blood
Could I be born again . . .
And yet
One night
In the tall black shadow
Of a windy pine
I offered up

The Sacrifice of Body
Upon the altar
Of her breast . . .
You
Who were conceived
Without ecstasy
Or pain
Can you understand
That I knelt last night
In Your House
And ate of Your Body
And drank of Your Blood.
. . . and thought only of her?

To James:
Do you remember
How you won
That last race . . . ?
How you flung your body
At the start . . .
How your spikes
Ripped the cinders
In the stretch . . .
How you catapulted
Through the tape . . .
Do you remember . . . ?
Don't you think
I lurched with you
Out of those starting holes . . . ?
Don't you think
My sinews tightened
At those first

Few strides . . .
And when you flew into the stretch
Was not all my thrill
Of a thousand races
In your blood . . . ?
At your final drive
Through the finish line
Did not my shout
Tell of the
Triumphant ecstasy
Of victory . . . ?
Live
As I have taught you
To run, Boy—
It's a short dash
Dig your starting holes
Deep and firm
Lurch out of them
Into the straightaway
With all the power
That is in you
Look straight ahead
To the finish line
Think only of the goal
Run straight
Run high
Run hard
Save nothing
And finish
With an ecstatic burst
That carries you
Hurtling

Through the tape
To victory. . . .

ON SEEING TWO BROWN BOYS IN A CATHOLIC CHURCH

It is fitting that you be here,
Little brown boys
With Christ-like eyes
And curling hair.

Look you on yon crucifix
Where He hangs nailed and pierced
With head hung low
And eyes a'blind with blood that drips
From a thorny crown . . .
Look you well,
You shall know this thing.

Judas' kiss will burn your cheek
And you shall be denied
By your Peter—
And Gethsemane . . .
You shall know full well
Gethsemane . . .

You, too, will suffer under Pontius Pilate
And feel the rugged cut of rough hewn cross
Upon your surging shoulder—
They will spit in your face
And laugh . . .
They will nail you up twixt thieves
And gamble for your little garments.

And in this you will exceed God
For on this earth
You shall know Hell—

O little brown boys
With Christ-like eyes
And curling hair
It is fitting that you be here.

TOAST

Here's to your eyes
for the things I see
drowned in them.
Here's to your lips
Two livid streaks of flame. . . .
Here's to your heart
May it ever be full
of the love of loving. . . .
Here's to your body
a lithesome hill top tree
swaying
to a spring's morning breath. . . .
Here's to your soul
as yet
unborn. . . .

TO A PERSISTENT PHANTOM

I buried you deeper last night
You with your tears
And your tangled hair
You with your lips

That kissed so fair
I buried you deeper last night.

I buried you deeper last night
With fuller breasts
And stronger arms
With softer lips
And newer charms
I buried you deeper last night.

Deeper . . . ay, deeper
And again tonight
Till that gay spirit
That once was you
Will tear its soul
In climbing through . . .
Deeper . . . ay, deeper
I buried you deeper last night.

IMMORTALITY

To be forever young
and ride like a tipsy Triton
on the crest of a wave
that is just forever breaking. . . .
Days—an eternal dawning
heralded with the fanfare of sun,
Nights—a blaze of glory
the swishing tail of a comet,
Life—an infinite loving
Sweeping to the peak of anticipation
Trembling breathlessly at the brink
of realization. . . .

HELENE JOHNSON

Helene Johnson *was born in Boston and was educated in the public schools of that city and at Boston University. In 1926 she came to New York and did some work in the Extension Division of Columbia University. Her poems then began to appear in* Opportunity, Vanity Fair, *and several other publications. This earliest work bore the stamp of a genuine poet. She is one of the younger group who has taken, so to speak, the "racial" bull by the horns. She has taken the very qualities and circumstances that have long called for apology or defense and extolled them in an unaffected manner. A number of her best poems are done in colloquial style—a style which numberless poets of this new age have assumed to be easy; she realizes the hard fact that an effective poem in colloquial style demands as much work and workmanship as a well-wrought sonnet. Miss Johnson also possesses true lyric talent.*

POEM

Little brown boy,
Slim, dark, big-eyed,
Crooning love songs to your banjo
Down at the Lafayette—
Gee, boy, I love the way you hold your head,
High sort of and a bit to one side,
Like a prince, a jazz prince. And I love
Your eyes flashing, and your hands,
And your patent-leathered feet,

And your shoulders jerking the jig-wa.
And I love your teeth flashing,
And the way your hair shines in the spotlight
Like it was the real stuff.
Gee, brown boy, I loves you all over.
I'm glad I'm a jig. I'm glad I can
Understand your dancin' and your
Singin', and feel all the happiness
And joy and don't-care in you.
Gee, boy, when you sing, I can close my ears
And hear tomtoms just as plain.
Listen to me, will you, what do I know
About tomtoms? But I like the word, sort of,
Don't you? It belongs to us.
Gee, boy, I love the way you hold your head,
And the way you sing and dance,
And everything.
Say, I think you're wonderful. You're
All right with me,
You are.

THE ROAD

Ah, little road, all whirry in the breeze,
A leaping clay hill lost among the trees,
The bleeding note of rapture streaming thrush
Caught in a drowsy bush
And stretched out in a single singing line of dusky song.
Ah, little road, brown as my race is brown,
Your trodden beauty like our trodden pride,
Dust of the dust, they must not bruise you down.
Rise to one brimming golden, spilling cry!

SONNET TO A NEGRO IN HARLEM

You are disdainful and magnificent—
Your perfect body and your pompous gait,
Your dark eyes flashing solemnly with hate,
Small wonder that you are incompetent
To imitate those whom you so despise—
Your shoulders towering high above the throng,
Your head thrown back in rich, barbaric song,
Palm trees and mangoes stretched before your eyes.
Let others toil and sweat for labor's sake
And wring from grasping hands their meed of gold.
Why urge ahead your supercilious feet?
Scorn will efface each footprint that you make.
I love your laughter arrogant and bold.
You are too splendid for this city street.

REMEMBER NOT

Remember not the promises we made
In this same garden many moons ago.
You must forget them. I would have it so.
Old vows are like old flowers as they fade
And vaguely vanish in a feeble death.
There is no reason why your hands should clutch
At pretty yesterdays. There is not much
Of beauty in me now. And though my breath
Is quick, my body sentient, my heart
Attuned to romance as before, you must
Not, through mistaken chivalry, pretend
To love me still. There is no mortal art
Can overcome Time's deep, corroding rust.
Let Love's beginning expiate Love's end.

INVOCATION

Let me be buried in the rain
In a deep, dripping wood,
Under the warm wet breast of Earth
Where once a gnarled tree stood.
And paint a picture on my tomb
With dirt and a piece of bough
Of a girl and a boy beneath a round, ripe moon
Eating of love with an eager spoon
And vowing an eager vow.
And do not keep my plot mowed smooth
And clean as a spinster's bed,
But let the weed, the flower, the tree,
Riotous, rampant, wild and free,
Grow high above my head.

WARING CUNEY

WARING CUNEY *was born in Washington, May 6, 1906. He was educated in the public schools of his native city and at Howard and Lincoln Universities. Later he went to Boston to study music. His poem "No Images" won first award in an* Opportunity *contest. He writes usually in free verse form with great economy of phrase; the best of his poems present clear, direct, and vivid images. His gift developed early and holds exceptional promise.*

NO IMAGES

She does not know
Her beauty,
She thinks her brown body
Has no glory.

If she could dance
Naked,
Under palm trees.
And see her image in the river
She would know.

But there are no palm trees
On the street,
And dish water gives back no images.

THRENODY

Only quiet death
Brings relief

From the wearisome
Interchange
Of hope and grief.
O body
(Credulous heart
And dream-torn head),
What will wisdom be
Or folly—
When you lie dead?
Life-beaten body
Bruised and sore—
Neither hunger nor satiety
Are known beyond death's door.

CONCEPTION

Jesus' mother never had no man.
God came to her one day an' said,
"Mary, chile, kiss ma han'."

TROUBLED JESUS

Ma Jesus
Was a troubled man,
Wid lots o' sorrow
In His breast.
Oh, he was weary
When they laid Him
In the tomb to rest.
Po', good Jesus.

CRUCIFIXION

They howled 'til Pilate
Sent dear Jesus out.
Then they cursed Him
An' knocked Him all about.

O brothers, O sisters,
Think what those sinners done—
Crucified the Lord's Son!
Think, think . . . Oh, think . . .

WAKE CRY

He was a good man.
All men have to die.

O Death,
Did you ever
Fall on your knees
In tears an' cry?

He was a good man,
Hear the widow moan.

O Death,
Do you weep—
Or is your heart
Made o' stone?

BURIAL OF THE YOUNG LOVE

Weep not,
You who love her.

Place your flowers
Above her
And go your way
Only I shall stay.

After you have gone
With grief in your hearts,
I will remove the flowers
You laid above her.
Yes, I who love her.

Do not weep,
Friends and lovers.

(Oh, the scent of flowers in the air!
Oh, the beauty of her body there!)

Gently now lay your flowers down.
When the last mourner has gone
And I have torn
Each flower;
When the last mourner has gone
And I have tossed
Broken stems and flower heads
To the winds . . . ah! . . .
I will gather withered leaves . . .
I will scatter withered leaves there.

Friends and lovers,
Do not weep.

Gently lay your flowers down . . .
Gently, now, lay your flowers down.

FINIS

Now that our love has drifted
To a quiet close,
Leaving the empty ache
That always follows when beauty goes;
Now that you and I,
Who stood tip-toe on earth
To touch our fingers to the sky,
Have turned away
To allow our little love to die—
Go, dear, seek again the magic touch.
But if you are wise,
As I shall be wise,
You will not again
Love over much.

LUCY ARIEL WILLIAMS

L UCY ARIEL WILLIAMS *was born in Mobile, Alabama, March 3, 1905. Her father was a physician in that city, and she had the advantage of being reared in a cultured home. She attended the public schools of her native city. In 1922 she was graduated from Talladega College. In 1926 she took the degree of Mus. B. at Fisk University. Later she pursued her musical studies at the Oberlin Conservatory. She is now director of music at North Carolina College for Negroes. Her poem "Northboun'" won first prize in the* Opportunity *contest for 1926 and brought her into notice as a poet.*

NORTHBOUN'

O' de wurl' ain't flat,
An' de wurl' ain't roun',
Hit's one long strip
Hangin' up an' down—
Jes' Souf an' Norf;
Jes' Norf an' Souf.

Talkin' 'bout sailin' 'roun' de wurl'—
Huh! I'd be so dizzy my head 'ud twurl
If dis heah earf wuz jes' a ball
You know the people all 'ud fall.

O' de wurl' ain't flat,
An' de wurl' ain't roun'.
Hit's one long strip
Hangin' up an' down—

Jes' Souf an' Norf;
Jes' Norf an' Souf.

Talkin' 'bout the City whut Saint John saw—
Chile, you oughta go to Saginaw;
A nigger's chance is "finest kind,"
An' pretty gals ain't hard to find.

Huh! de wurl' ain't flat,
An' de wurl' ain't roun',
Jes' one long strip
Hangin' up an' down.
Since Norf is up,
An' Souf is down,
An' Hebben is up,
I'm upward boun'.

APPENDIX

APPENDIX

PLÁCIDO'S SONNET TO HIS MOTHER

DESPIDA A MI MADRE

(En La Capilla)

Si la suerte fatal que me ha cabido,
Y el triste fin de mi sangrienta historia,
Al salir de esta vida transitoria
Deja tu corazon de muerte herido;
  Baste de llanto: el ánimo afligido
Recobre su quietud; moro en la gloria,
Y mi plácida lira á tu memoria
Lanza en la tumba su postrer sonido.

Sonido dulce, melodioso y santo,
Glorioso, espiritual, puro y divino,
Inocente, espontáneo como el llanto
  Que vertiera al nacer: ya el cuello inclino!
Ya de la religion me cubre el manto!
Adios, mi madre! adios—El Peligrino.

FAREWELL TO MY MOTHER

(In the Chapel)

The appointed lot has come upon me, mother,
The mournful ending of my years of strife,
This changing world I leave, and to another
In blood and terror goes my spirit's life.

But thou, grief-smitten, cease thy mortal weeping
And let thy soul her wonted peace regain;
I fall for right, and thoughts of thee are sweeping
Across my lyre to wake its dying strain.
   A strain of joy and gladness, free, unfailing,
All glorious and holy, pure, divine,
And innocent, unconscious as the wailing
   I uttered on my birth; and I resign
Even now, my life, even now descending slowly,
Faith's mantle folds me to my slumbers holy.
Mother, farewell! God keep thee—and forever!
       Translated by William Cullen Bryant.

PLÁCIDO'S FAREWELL TO HIS MOTHER
(*Written in the Chapel of the Hospital de Santa Cristina on the Night Before His Execution*)

   If the unfortunate fate engulfing me,
The ending of my history of grief,
The closing of my span of years so brief,
Mother, should wake a single pang in thee,
Weep not. No saddening thought to me devote;
I calmly go to a death that is glory-filled;
My lyre before it is forever stilled
Breathes out to thee its last and dying note.

A note scarce more than a burden-easing sigh,
Tender and sacred, innocent, sincere—
Spontaneous and instinctive as the cry
I gave at birth—And now the hour is here—
O God, thy mantle of mercy o'er my sins!
Mother, farewell! The pilgrimage begins.
       Translated by James Weldon Johnson.

BOOKS SUGGESTED FOR COLLATERAL READING

The Negro in Literature and Art. Benjamin Brawley. Duffield, New York.

A Bibliographical Checklist of American Negro Poetry. Arthur A. Schomburg. Heartmann, New York.

Caroling Dusk—an Anthology. Edited by Countee Cullen. Harper and Brothers, New York.

Prefaces to *The Book of American Negro Spirituals, The Second Book of American Negro Spirituals,* and *God's Trombones.* James Weldon Johnson. Viking Press, New York.

The New Negro. Edited by Alain Locke. A. and C. Boni, New York.

The Gift of Black Folk. W. E. B. Du Bois. The Stratford Company, Boston.

Negro Folk Rhymes. Thomas W. Talley, Macmillan, New York.

Negro Poets and Their Poems. Edited by Robert T. Kerlin. Associated Publishers, Washington.

An Anthology of Verse by American Negroes. Edited by Newman I. White and W. C. Jackson. Duke University Press, Durham, N. C.

Anthologies of Magazine Verse. W. S. Braithwaite.

The Negro in Contemporary American Literature. Elizabeth Lay Green. University of North Carolina Press.

An Anthology of American Negro Literature. Edited by V. F. Calverton. The Modern Library.

Ebony and Topaz. Charles S. Johnson. Opportunity, New York.

Four Negro Poets. Edited by Alain Locke. Simon and Schuster, New York.

Modern American Poetry. Edited by Louis Untermeyer. Harcourt, Brace and Company, New York.

Our Singing Strength. Alfred Kreymborg. Coward-McCann, New York.

Hunters of Heaven. Clement Wood. Frederick A. Stokes, New York.

Poets of America. Clement Wood. Dutton, New York.

The Advancing South. Edwin Mims. Doubleday, New York.

Folk Songs of the American Negro. J. W. Work. Fisk University Press.

The Negro and His Songs. Howard W. Odum and Guy B. Johnson. University of North Carolina Press.

Negro Workaday Songs. Howard W. Odum and Guy B. Johnson. University of North Carolina Press.

On the Trail of Negro Folk Songs. Dorothy Scarborough. Harvard University Press.

Blues—An Anthology. W. C. Handy and Abbé Niles. A. and C. Boni, New York.

Singing Soldiers. John J. Niles. Scribner, New York.

INDEX OF AUTHORS

INDEX OF TITLES